THE BUSINESS CASE ROADMAP – BCR:

how to use the Business Case to expand your business and avoid pitfalls

THE BUSINESS CASE ROADMAP – BCR:

how to use the Business Case to expand your business and avoid pitfalls

2019

Vitor Verdelho Vieira
Susana Costa e Silva

ACTUAL

TÍTULO:
The business case roadmap – BCR. How to use the Business Case to expand your business and avoid pitfalls

AUTORES
Susana Costa Silva e Vitor Verdelho Vieira

CONJUNTURA ACTUAL EDITORA
Sede: Rua Fernandes Tomás, 76-80, 3000-167 Coimbra
Delegação: LEAP CENTER – Espaço Amorciras
Rua D. João V, n.º 24, 1.03
1250-091 Lisboa – Portugal
e-mail: editoras@grupoalmedina.net

CAPA
FBA

PAGINAÇÃO
Aresta Criativa – Artes Gráficas

IMPRESSÃO E ACABAMENTO:
ARTIPOL - www.artipol.net
Outubro 2019

DEPÓSITO LEGAL
462816/19

ACTUAL | GRUPOALMEDINA

BIBLIOTECA NACIONAL DE PORTUGAL – CATALOGAÇÃO NA PUBLICAÇÃO
SILVA, Susana Costa e, e outro

The business case roadmap – BCR. How to use the Business Case to expand your business and avoid pitfalls/ Susana Costa e Silva, Vítor Verdelho Vieira. – (Fora de coleção)
ISBN 978-989-694-308-0

I – VIEIRA, Vítor Verdelho

CDU 005

What to expect?

Dear reader, before we start we would like to inform you about what your expectation should be, regarding the contents of this book. In a moment when being an entrepreneur seems to be popular, one my think this is a condition to succeed professionally. However that is not always the case. Many people desire to start a business, but only some actually do it.

We believe that every person has a certain level of inherent entrepreneurship. However, this is shown in different levels and different contexts. Not everyone is made to be a typical entrepreneur and not all the business that entrepreneurs start are faded to be a success. In the process to turn a passion or an idea into a great business, there are guidelines that deserve to be followed and expectations that need to be managed. This is (also) what this book is about.

It is ***not*** *possible* to teach you ***how to be*** an entrepreneur. However you can learn how to be a better entrepreneur. The entrepreneur's **attitude** is something that is possible to develop and consolidate with knowledge and skills, even though it is **not** possible to obtain in a learning course.

It **is** possible to learn ***business development*** only by analogy, with examples and case studies, **but** that has a very limited outcome. Premature conclusions or wrong validation procedures can lead to misleading conclusions. Furthermore, the lack of doing the validation, when ideas are consolidated, can also lead to a global failure. A second and third opinion or mentoring are a best practice. This is also what this book is about.

It **is** possible to have a **sustainable business** without a team where leadership and multiple skills are centred in a single person. However this would be a very unlikely situation. To develop a business is different from developing a business idea. Execution is very different from ideation and it requires different resources. Resources and a good team are both necessary and important. As a matter of fact The Team is the most important factor for success and the 'Business Case Roadmap' (BCR) is centered in this concept.

What is this book about?

The 'BUSINESS CASE roadmap' (The BCR) collection presents a step-by-step procedure to find possible paths for the establishment of a business. *The roadmap follows an algorithm that is based on* ***a logical sequence of operations, according to heuristic concepts and best practices.*** Frequently people have good ideas for business and in several cases, they follow them to start testing a business. This has proven to be a wrong approach when for instance, the wrong questions are asked in a market survey and, as a result, the idea can be killed before even being born. As a matter of fact, there is a wide range of possible paths that an idea can lead to. However, some of them are better than others and some can even be destructive. Chance frequently plays a relevant role in the choice of paths, but relying on chance can lead to uncertain results, which we would like to avoid. For the construction of this tool, we base on best practices observed throughout years of experience in conducting business.

Each idea and each **business team** can follow an algorithm with a specific path or roadmap, based on a global sequence of interrelated steps, which can vary from business to business. This roadmap should be considered with a clear understanding of the different alternatives available. New business set-ups, existing business development or franchising can follow The BCR, which turns this process useful in different situation and widens its scope of action.

The BCR is **not** an academic approach, but rather a collated aggregation of entrepreneurs' visions, based on their knowledge and experience. Key concepts and definitions are used, to turn complex topics into easy ones and order to facilitate the understanding and use of concepts that represent the state-of-the-art in business development. We believe that following the proposed algorithm will lead to the highest predictable chances of success.

For a global approach to business development, we will present three volumes for this collection. In the first one we will explain how to evolve from the Idea to the Business Case; in the second one we will explain the go-to-market and how to navigate in the implementation stage; in the third one, we will focus on how to expand the business, avoid common mistakes inherent to this stage; and we will also emphasize the financial backup required for the expansion of the operation.

About the authors

Who are we?

VITOR VERDELHO VIEIRA is mentor of several companies that he co-founded with partners in different sectors. He started his first biotech company - Necton, SA - www.necton.pt in March 1989, which is now a European leader in the production and sale of traditional sea salt and fleur de sel, as well as the production of microalgae for aquaculture and cosmetics. He is also co-founder of A4F - Algae for Future, SA - www.a4f.pt an international reference company in the sector of microalgae technologies. He is the General Manager of EABA the European Algae Biomass Association, with headquarters in Florence. His business experience is wide and ranges from engineering consulting and real estate to biotechnology and medical devices. In the different companies, he developed and participated in more than 40 R&D projects along the last 25 years and interacted with more than 200 different organizations in Europe. Between 2000 and 2015 he has been involved in the management of SpinLogic the entrepreneurship programme and business Incubator from the Universidade Católica Portuguesa in Porto, where he followed and supported more than 150 projects. He is presently visiting professor in Católica Porto Business School and School of Arts in the same University. He has a background in Physics from the University of Porto, Faculty of Sciences and established his management knowledge through more than a dozen specialized training courses in Portugal and abroad in the last 30 years. More information can be found at: https://pt.linkedin.com/in/vitorverdelho

SUSANA COSTA E SILVA has a Ph.D. in Marketing from University College de Dublin (Ireland), a MSc. in Economics from Faculty of Economics in University of Porto and she is graduated in Management at Universidade Católica Portuguesa. She is Associated Professor at Católica Porto Business School (CPBS) since 1997. She is the coordinator of the MSc in Marketing and of the MSc in Management at CPBS. She is also Researcher at CEGE (Research Centre in Management and Economics) and Member of CEGEA (Research Center in Management and Applied Economics). Along the years, she supervised more than 100 thesis. Susana authored several books and book chapters published in Portugal, UK, USA, Brazil and China in the fields of marketing and international marketing, cooperation and international alliances. She has been presenting her academic researches in international conferences in the fields of marketing, consumer behavior and international business. She publishes in international journals in the same fields. Susana is also active as consultant in marketing and international business. She writes regularly in Portuguese magazines and newspapers. She is visiting scholar in universities in Brazil, China and Poland. She is national representative for Portugal at the European Marketing Academy and she was during 6 years national representative for Portugal at European International Business Academy. More information can be found at: http://www.porto.ucp.pt/pt/cv-susana-silva

What are our motivations?

We want to transform our combined knowledge and experience, resulting from a diversified set of sources, in a useful tool that can be used by entrepreneurs, managers and business students. Through-out the years we directly accessed more than 300 new business, to which we have studied and surveyed 300 other from literature. We found useful to present our views on the analysis conducted along the years and systematize relevant insights from this into a series of 'best practices' in a compact and very direct way.

Following a 'question and answer' methodology we believe to have been able to establish a possible algorithm for the development of a 'Business Case'. This was validated and tested with a wide number of MBA students and entrepreneurs. On the basis of this validation it was possible to find that this approach is effective and innovative, thus providing an easy and fast learning process.

The BUSINESS CASE roadmap aims at providing a guided learning, where the tools and clues for a deeper exploratory work with interpretation of examples and case studies, is suggested. Each individual and each team can benefit from this book differently: each person will have a specific topic and relevant examples to evaluate and can develop a different interpretation on the arguments provided.

WE CAN'T
DIRECT THE WIND.
BUT WE CAN
ADJUST THE SAILS.

- THOMAS S. MONSON -

Table of contents

Introduction 17

Why an algorithmic logic? 19

1. What is the 'life cycle' of companies? Why is it important for growth? 21
2. What is the role of strategy in business expansion? 27
3 How to develop a strategic programme for business expansion? 37
4. How to find, deal with and manage investors? 45
5. What are the best practices for raising money for a developing business? 53
6. How are investment rounds organised and how are they used? 63
7. What is the evolution process from startup, to scale up and scaler? 73
8. Why do some companies grow faster? 81
9. Why do some companies live longer? 87
10. What are gazelle companies? And what can we learn from them? 95
11. What are unicorn companies? And what can we learn from them? 99
12. What are the common characteristics of inspiring and fast-growing companies? 105
13. What are the most common business failure factors? 113
14. How can disruptive business models be adapted for any business? 121

15. What are the drivers for the International Marketing Plan? 131
16. How to combine exports with international business development? 137
17. How can 'value chain analyses' be used for business development? 143
18. What are the main challenges in developing a business? . 149
19. What are the main business management and business strategy mistakes? How can they be avoided? 157
20. How to sell a business? 165
21. Concluding remarks 179

Introduction

The **BUSINESS CASE roadmap** presents a step-by-step procedure to achieve the establishment of a business, according to a logical sequence of operations, based on best practices and heuristic concepts. There is a wide range of possible options an entrepreneur may take during the development of a business idea. Some of these are better than others, and some can even be destructive.

The level of success is uncertain and chance often plays an important role. However, best practices can help to find the algorithm that works out the highest predictable chances of success for each business. Hence, each idea and each business team will be challenged to follow a specific path based on a global sequence of interrelated and variable steps. A new business set-up, the developing of an existing business or even a franchising model, can all follow the algorithm.

We would like to highlight that The **BUSINESS CASE roadmap** is not an academic approach, but rather a collection of entrepreneurial visions, based on knowledge and experience. Key concepts and definitions will be used, to turn complex topics into simple ones, and to understand and use state-of-the-art concepts in business development. Sometimes the same concept is repeated along different frameworks.

The third volume in the collection describes the steps involved in expanding the business, avoiding common mistakes that are characteristic of this stage and gaining/understanding/assessing the financial backing required in order to expand the operation.

The 'Business Case' is an operational tool, developed by the project team, which describes a set of statements and responds to the critical questions that define the business and its development. Typically, a two-page document, it works as a summary of the execution of the business plan. It is a compact and flexible document that is shared with the team and that can be adapted step by step, as the business evolves and adjusts to the competitive environment and market needs. The business case is more a compact guide than a business plan but can be expanded to become a business plan, if required.

Why an algorithmic logic?

An algorithm "is a sequence of instructions telling us what to do"; algorithms are reducible to logical operations that can be interrelated. Following a 'question and answer' methodology, we can establish a possible algorithm for the development of a 'business case'. After testing it with a large number of MBA students and entrepreneurs, we have found this approach to be effective and innovative, providing an easier learning process. The specific questions being considered represent the most common questions asked by students and by entrepreneurs starting new businesses. The answers are based on best practices and academic information about reference concepts and definitions.

Before starting the business development process, it is critical to understand why we have chosen a specific path and specific options. When we do, the process flows in a logical and natural way.

The responses to such questions as *who? what? why? when? where? how?* and *how much?* require a clear understanding of the business, and this results in an effective way to communicate the project to all those who are interested in it. By following this method, we are exposed to a dichotomous way of thinking that can provide an easier set of options and a pathway to the Business Case roadmap.

The dichotomous thinking approach is a simplified way of distinguishing between different options. There are always several possible options and paths that could be followed. It is critical to know in advance, what the options are, and why they should be considered, so that it is possible to choose the one, which is considered the best in the specific context of the team, resources and time scale. The ability to create dichotomy makes the process a great deal smoother.

Planning is mandatory but if done without previous development and appropriate tools, it might kill the idea from the start.

Many businesses fail for lack of planning and many business die because of a lack of planning and the subsequent misuse of resources.

Rather than simply using an algorithmic logic, it is helpful to use information about predictable futures and best practices regarding options for evolutionary growth. Where patterns exist, we can learn from them, and anticipate potential outcomes.

1

What is the 'life cycle' of companies? Why is it important for growth?

What is a company's life cycle?

The *life cycle* of a business is its progression and different phases over time. All collective organisations - as is the case with living organisms - evolve through a series of predictable phases, which we call the *life cycle* [1]. This is most commonly divided into several stages: introduction, growth, maturity and decline, or, alternatively: launch, growth, shake-out, maturity, and decline.

To anticipate the future and then manage accordingly is critical for the sustainable expansion of a business. While we cannot predict the future in detail, by looking ahead, we know roughly what to expect. We can do this by studying company's life cycle, using a global yearly approach (see page 36 of The BCR, Vol. 1), and/or on the basis of a study of the individual firm's short weekly or monthly life cycles, which are related to time management (see page 27 of The BCR 2).

Why it is important to know and understand company life cycles?

Organisations go through predictable patterns of growth and development. If we are able to forecast the future, we can manage things accordingly. As an organisation grows, its personality (and culture) changes. Its focus, priorities, problems, concerns and complexity also change. This life cycle involves a series of phases of evolutionary growth followed by crisis, which eventually requires revolutionary growth of the organisation and/or its people, followed by another period of evolutionary growth, and so on. This evolution can be understood in detail using the Greiner Growth Model (see below).

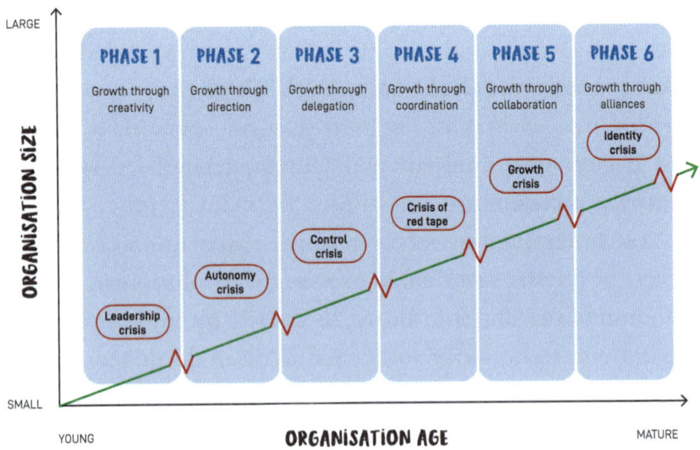

Source: adapted from www.toolshero.com, consulted in 28/4/2019.

The Greiner Growth Model is a very important contribution to our understanding of the possible steps and strategies involved in business expansion. It is a simple yet valuable tool for business planning.

Larry Greiner (1933) is Professor Emeritus of Management and Organization at the University of Southern California. He is especially famous for his development of the Greiner Growth Model for organisations. This strategic management model has five phases of organisational development that are accompanied by growing pains and resistance.

Larry Greiner supported several faculties as a director and as a teacher. He has also lectured at the Harvard Business School, the University of Kansas (United States), University of Oxford (United Kingdom), and INSEAD in Fontainebleau (France).

What are the drivers of a company life cycle?

The drivers of a company's life cycle depend strongly on the type of business in question. The main factor relates to the role of technology in the business. More intensely tech-driven businesses tend to have stronger evolutionary traits, higher diversity and shorter cycles.

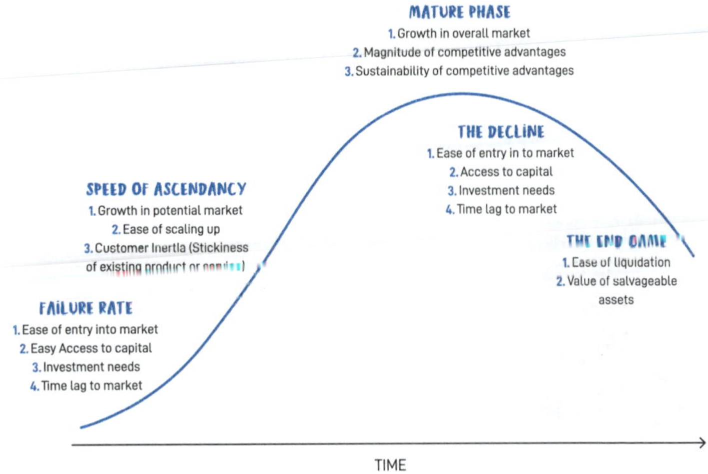

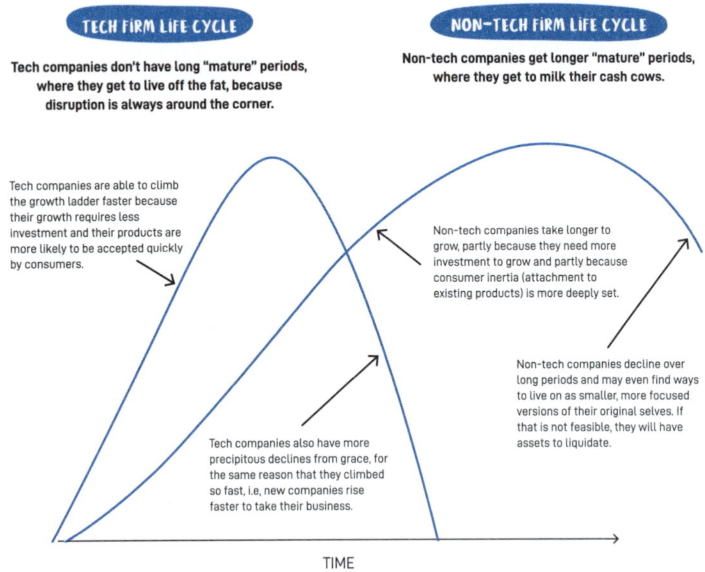

Source: adapted from: www.valuewalk.com/2015/12/tech-life-cycle/, consulted in 29/7/2019.

What are the options at the life cycle *tipping point*?

At a certain moment (the tipping point), the accumulation of small changes or incidents may become significant enough to cause a larger, more important change. At this point, organisations have three options:

1. Reinvent themselves and evolve
2. Decline, decay and die
3. Integrate with another organisation.

The fate of a small company is either to grow and become a large company, to disappear, or to be part of an M&A process. Mergers and Acquisitions are often an important part of many organisations. In many cases, reinvention and growth can occur through the acquisition of another organisation or business (See The BCR Vol. 1, page 36, which expands on this point).

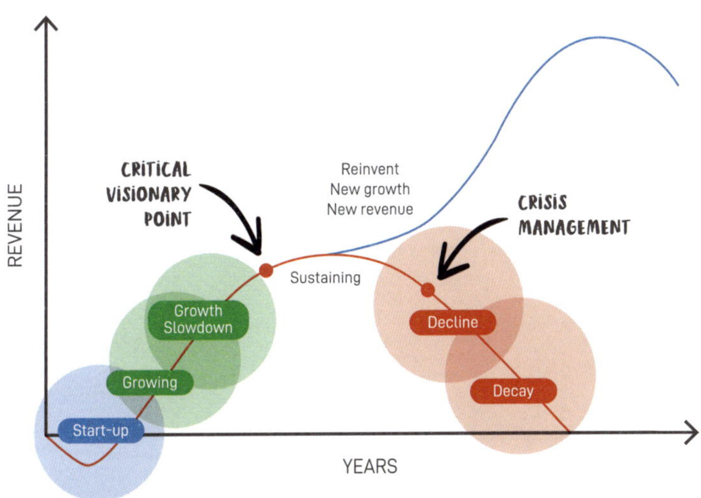

What is the most important decision to start with?

The most important prerequisite, when it comes to scaling a business, is to have good advisers or consultants to help with the strategic options, including the investment strategy. Good consultants can provide smart advice and can act as mediators with investors and even prospective customers. The selection of consultants is a critical process and should be focused on finding trustworthy partners with knowledge and experience that can be verified through due diligence.

KEY IDEAS AND REFERENCES FOR MORE INFORMATION

- The understanding of business life cycles allows us to predict the future
- To be successful, you have to take the right steps at the right time
- Growth is not a linear pattern and cycles exist and can be managed

[1] MacArthur, R., and Wilson, E. O. (2001) The Theory of Island Biogeography (Vol. 1). Princeton University Press.

[2] Greiner, L. E. (1998). Evolution and revolution as organizations grow. Harvard business review, 76(3), 55-64.

[3] Gilkey, C. (2014) The Small Business Life Cycle: The No-Fluff Guide to Navigating the Five Stages of Small Business Growth. Kindle Edition.

[4] Gersick,K. E., Davis, J. A., Hampton, M. M. and Lansberg, I. (1997). Generation to Generation: Life Cycles of the Family Business. Harvard Business Press.

2

What is the role of strategy in business expansion?

What is a business expansion strategy?

Business expansion strategy, or growth strategy, is the method, which a company uses in order to expand or grow its business. It depends largely on the organisation's financial situation, the competition, and even on government regulation. There are three types of possible growth strategies. They can be combined in different ways and sequences and used simultaneously and at different levels.

Organic growth	Partnerships growth	Acquisition-based growth
The four Product-Market strategies	Strategic alliances, Joint ventures, Franchising	Competitors, Suppliers, Distributors
Internal development logics	Cooperation logics	Integration logics

What is organic growth and what is the Ansoff Matrix?

Organic growth is the growth rate a company can achieve by increasing output and enhancing sales internally. The best-known tool for strategic management and organic business expansion is the Ansoff Matrix. This matrix presents the different options according to a set of logical possibilities. This framework can be useful for both new and long-established businesses.

The Ansoff Matrix - also known as Ansoff's product and market growth matrix - is a planning tool, which usually aids a business in determining its product and market growth, either for strategy definition, or for implementation. When we talk about the growing, we should think about our products and our markets. 'Product', it can refer to either an actual Product or a Service. This is usually determined by focusing on whether the products are new or existing, and whether the market is new or existing. The Ansoff Matrix contains four alternative marketing strategies: market penetration, product development, market development and diversification.

Market Penetration. The first quadrant in Ansoff's matrix is market penetration. This means that in order to grow, the organisation may have to go out of its way to increase market share. This is often adopted as a strategy when the organisation has an existing product with a known market and needs a growth strategy within that market. In essence, it involves selling more of the same, which requires a powerful marketing strategy.

Market Development. Market development is the second market growth strategy in Ansoff's matrix. This strategy is used when the firm targets a new market with existing products. For a smaller firm, this strategy includes expanding from a current market to another market, where its product does not currently compete. Internationalisation strategies can be considered here.

Product Development. Product development in the Ansoff matrix refers to businesses that have a good market share in an existing market and therefore might need to introduce new products for expansion. Product development is needed when the company has a good customer base and knows that the market for its existing product has reached saturation. A new product development strategy that caters to the existing market may be considered a good approach. In this case, the market penetration strategy is no longer practical.

Diversification. The diversification strategy in Ansoff's matrix applies when the product is completely new and is being introduced into a new market. This is the most risky approach of the four, as both the market and the product are new to the firm.

Igor Ansoff (1918- 2002) was a prominent Russian American mathematician and scientist. He is known as the father of strategic management, and for his development of the strategy model, the Ansoff matrix. Ansoff was primarily a mathematician with an expert insight into business management. The concept of strategic management is widely attributed to him.

After this study and his research activities, Igor Ansoff joined the UCL Senior Executive Program. He was a distinguished professor and carried out research in the area of strategic management for several institutes for 17 years. In addition to being a professor, Igor Ansoff was an advisor, and he consulted with hundreds of multinational corporations including IBM, Philips, General Electric, Sterling and Westinghouse with respect to strategic management.

The four strategic options described by Ansoff's matrix can be obtained by organic growth, networking and/or acquisition strategies. Very often strategic business plans combine several possibilities to formulate a global masterplan for business development.

What are partnership growth strategies?

Partnership-based growth can have a wide range of configurations, from strategic alliance partnerships to franchising.

Strategic alliances	Joint ventures	Franchising
Typically project-based	*Typically venture-based*	*Typically large-network-based*
A common growth strategy is to pursue partnerships with other companies. A partnership can be as simple as an informal agreement - made between businesses in complementary markets - to refer clients to one another. Through a strategic alliance, two companies will decide to share resources to accomplish a specific, mutually beneficial project. A strategic alliance is a strategic cooperation between two or more orga-nisations, with the aim of achieving a result that one of the parties cannot achieve alone.	More complex partnerships include **joint ventures**, in which two or more businesses pool resources to develop a common project. A joint venture can be considered a new organisational and legal entity, legally separate from the parent firms, who created it and jointly participate as co-owners. Management is normally shared among the different partners that make up the joint venture.	Franchising can be a successful growth strategy, especially if there is a profitable operation that can be easily replicated by others. It can be complex but is a good option for fast growth. Such a business usually comes with name recognition, serious marketing power and support from the franchise owner. Due diligence in investigating all costs - including start-up fees, royalties, adver-tising and supplies - is critical. This is a good way to learn and get business insights.

What is acquisition-based growth strategy?

Buying another company through an **acquisition** strategy can be a cost-effective way to increase market share, capture new markets or diversify. This strategy provides an established clientele and operation, which can be adjusted to add value. Acquisition may be a good strategy if the firm wants to expand into a new geographic location or to another country where contacts and local knowledge are lacking. Proper due diligence must be conducted to evaluate any opportunity.

Competitor acquisition	**Supplier acquisition**	**Diversification acquisition**
Horizontal integration	*Vertical integration*	*Forward integration*
When a company wishes to grow through horizontal integration, its aim is to acquire a similar company in the same industry. Companies may choose to undergo horizontal integration in order to increase their size, diversify their product or service offerings, achieve economies of scale, or reduce competition. They may also wish to gain access to new customers or markets, including those overseas. For example, a supermarket chain may choose to merge with a similar one in another country to start operations abroad. The result of horizontal integration, when successful, is the ability to produce more revenue together compared to if the two companies were to compete independently. In addition to this, a newly-merged company can cut down on costs by sharing technology, marketing, research and development (R&D), production, and distribution.	A company that undergoes vertical integration acquires a company that operates in the production process or value chain of the same industry. Some of the reasons companies do this include strengthening their supply chain, reducing production costs, capturing upstream or downstream profits, or accessing new distribution channels. To do this, one company acquires another that is either upstream or downstream in the supply chain process. Backward integration occurs when a company decides to buy another company that makes an input product for the acquiring company's product. For example, a car manufacturer undergoes backward integration if it acquires a tyre manufacturer. This move ensures the manufacturer has a steady supply of tyres in order to keep making its cars. Forward integration occurs when a company decides to take control of the post-production process. For example, a footwear producer may decide to acquire a shoe shop through forward integration – the process of acquiring a business which is in front of its own supply chain. This not only gets the manufacturer closer to the consumer, but it also gives the company more revenue.	Diversification happens when a company acquires a company in a different sector. This acquisition can refer to companies in different sectors. It involves more risk as the new company operates in a business sector that is new to the acquiring firm.

How can we define and rank the parameters for the options?

Any future business must be sustainable. The best practice in deciding on options is to apply sustainability criteria. This means developing a diagnosis for the different options and ranking them according to sustainability criteria. Sustainable development was defined by the Brundtland Commission of the United Nations in 1987. Since then the sustainability movement is guided by the three commonly referred to as the "three pillars" of sustainability: environment, economics, and social. The metrics used for the measurement of sustainability are still evolving; they include indicators, benchmarks, audits, indexes and accounting, as well as assessment, appraisal and other reporting systems.

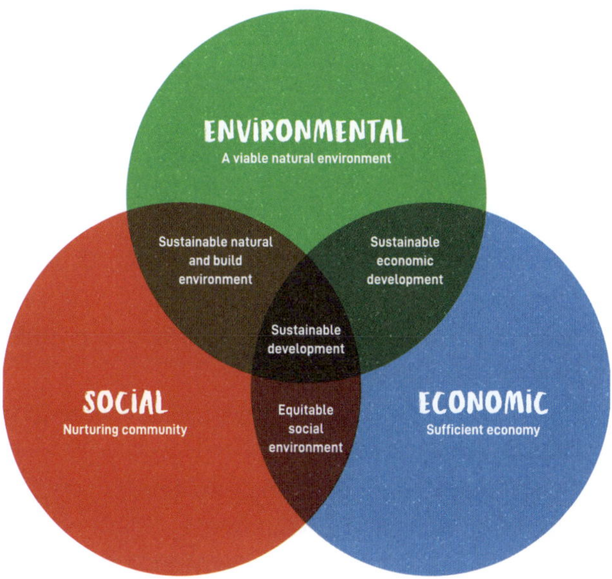

There are two methodologies that business can evaluate and compare to rank sustainability criteria:

(1) Triple bottom line (TBL) accounting that expands the traditional reporting framework to take into account social and environmental performance in addition to financial performance. Some organisations have adopted the TBL framework to evaluate their performance from a broader perspective to create greater business value.

(2) Circles of Sustainability. This is a method for understanding and assessing sustainability, and for managing projects directed towards socially sustainable outcomes. This approach has a higher focus on social issues.

What is the process for deciding on strategic options?

It is important to follow a structured logic for the business expansion strategy:

1. Evaluate the possible option in as much detail as possible
2. Develop checklists for the analysis of the different options (see the BCR, Vol. 2)
3. Establish a ranking of priorities and prerequisites/conditions for the options
4. Define a set of contingential situations
5. Develop a strategic programme

Proper analytics regarding the framework of strategic options will provide immense help in dealing with the unexpected, and with the need for quick decisions. This is where "doing your homework" really pays!

KEY IDEAS AND REFERENCES FOR MORE INFORMATION

- The Ansoff matrix provides a simple and powerful tool for the definition of strategic options.
- Business growth can happen through three different alternatives: organic, through partnerships and through acquisitions.
- Partnerships are threefold: strategic alliances, joint ventures and franchising.
- There are three types of acquisitions: competitors' acquisitions, suppliers' acquisitions and diversification.
- Sustainability is measured through three criteria: economic, environmental and social. Sustainability is a mandatory criteria in the evaluation of strategic options.

[1] Ansoff, I. (1988) The New Corporate Strategy, John Wiley & Sons, New York, NY.
[2] Sroufe, R. P. (2018) Integrated Management: How Sustainability Creates Value for Any Business. Emerald Publishing Limited.
[3] Langert, B. (2019) The Battle to Do Good. Emerald Publishing Limited.
[4] Bernard J. Jaworski and Robert S. Lurie (2018) The Organic Growth Playbook: Activate High-Yield Behaviors To Achieve Extraordinary Results—Every Time (American Marketing Association Leadership Series: 7 Big Problems of Marketing)
[5] Herriott, S. R. (2016) Metrics for Sustainable Business: Measures and Standards for the Assessment of Organizations. Routledge.
[6] Hague, P. (2019) The Business Models Handbook: Templates, Theory and Case Studies. Kogan Page Publishers.

3

How to develop a strategic programme for business expansion

Why is it important to start with an evaluation of our competitors?

A strategic programme should start with a very detailed evaluation of the business situation of competitors. A growth strategy involves learning from competitors and understanding their success factors, so that it is possible to emulate them. Knowledge about competitors is at once a source of inspiration and an important asset to develop defence mechanisms and tactical actions in the marketplace (see Vol. 1, BCR).

How to develop a 'simple' competitor evaluation?

Good practice - followed by many business, sectors, cities, regions, and even countries - has been to use the Porter Five

Forces Model. This model can be summarised in a 'simple' map, but requires a background of detailed supporting information. A good suggestion would be to adapt the diagram below.

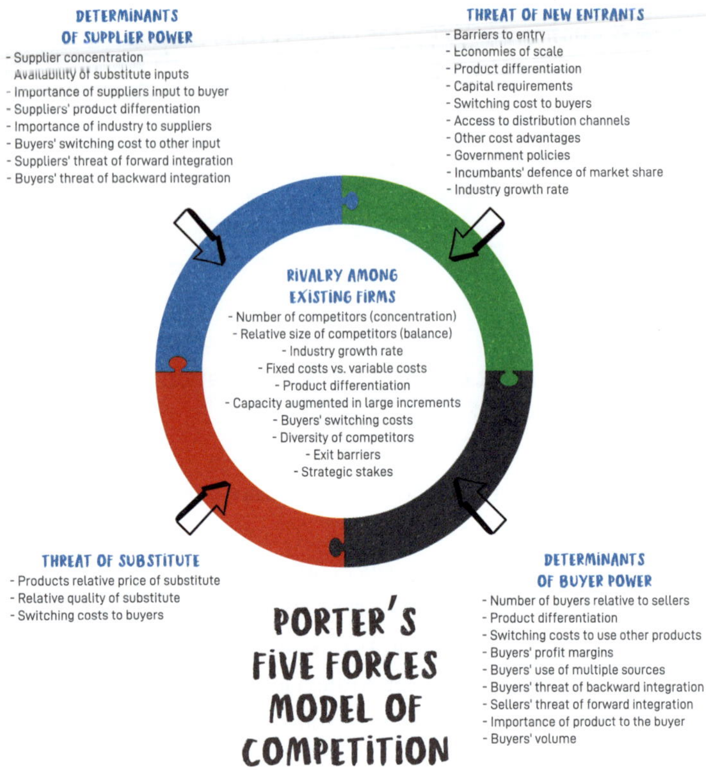

Michael Porter (1947-present) is professor and a management guru in the field of competitive strategy. He is the Department Head of Harvard Business School (HBS) and he was one of the founders of the consulting firm The Monitor Group, and FSG, a social impact consultancy. The Competitive Forces Model (or 'Five Forces Model'), the Value Chain Model, the Porter Diamond Model and the theories on Generic Strategies that were developed by him are known worldwide at every level of management.

Some of his most famous quotes are: "The essence of strategy is choosing what not to do"; "Strategy is the creation of an unique and valuable position, involving a different set of activities"; Strategy requires you to make trade-offs in competing – to choose what not to do"; "Innovation is the central issue in economic prosperity".

How to evolve from a red ocean to a blue ocean strategy?

W. Chan Kim and Renée Mauborgne coined the terms 'red ocean' and 'blue ocean' to denote a specific market universe. Red oceans are all the industries in existence today – the known market space, where industry boundaries are defined and companies try to outperform their rivals to grab a greater share of the existing market. This is cutthroat competition that turns the ocean blood-red - hence the term 'red' oceans. Blue ocean strategy is a totally different in approach. It involves the simultaneous pursuit of differentiation and low cost to open up a new market space and create new demand. It is about creating and capturing uncontested market space, thereby making the competition irrelevant. Blue ocean is therefore an analogy for the wider, deeper potential of market space that is not yet explored.

WHAT ARE RED OCEANS? Red oceans are all the industries in existence today – the known market space	**WHAT ARE BLUE OCEANS?** Blue oceans are all the industries not in existence today – the unknown market space.
WHY DO WE CALL THEM RED OCEANS? Cut-throat competition in existing industries turns the ocean blood-red. Hence the term 'red ocean'.	WHY DO WE CALL THEM BLUE OCEANS? Unexplored and untainted by competition, 'blue oceans' are vast, deep and powerful in terms of opportunity and growth.
WHAT IS RED OCEAN STRATEGY? Red ocean strategy is all about competition. As the market space gets more crowded, companies compete fiercely for a greater share of limited demand.	WHAT IS BLUE OCEAN STRATEGY? Blue ocean strategy creates new demand. Companies develop uncontested market space rather than fight over a shrinking profit pool.
WHAT OUTCOMES DOES RED OCEAN STRATEGY PRODUCE? Competing in red oceans is a zero-sum game. A market-competing strategy divides existing wealth between rival companies. As competition increases, prospects for profit and growth decline.	WHAT OUTCOMES DOES BLUE OCEAN STRATEGY PRODUCE? Creating blue oceans is non-zero-sum. There is ample opportunity for growth that is both profitable and rapid.
Compete in existing market space.	Create uncontested market space.
Beat the competition.	Make the competition irrelevant.
Exploit existing demand.	Create and capture new demand.
Make the value-cost trade-off.	Break the value-cost trade-off.
Align the whole system of a firm's activities with its strategic choice of differentiation or low cost.	Align the whole system of a firm's activities in pursuit of differentiation and low cost.

Source: adapted from: www.blueoceanstrategy.com/what-are-red-blue-oceans/, consulted in 23/8/2019.

Value innovation is the simultaneous pursuit of differentiation and low cost, creating value for both the buyer, the company, and its employees, thereby opening up new and uncontested market space.

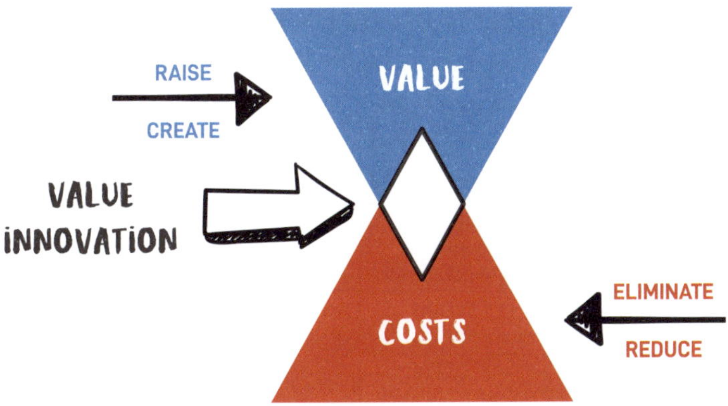

To operate the value innovation approach, it is crucial to understand which of the firm's activities are to be eliminated, reduced, and raised and which ones need to be created so as to explore new market potential.

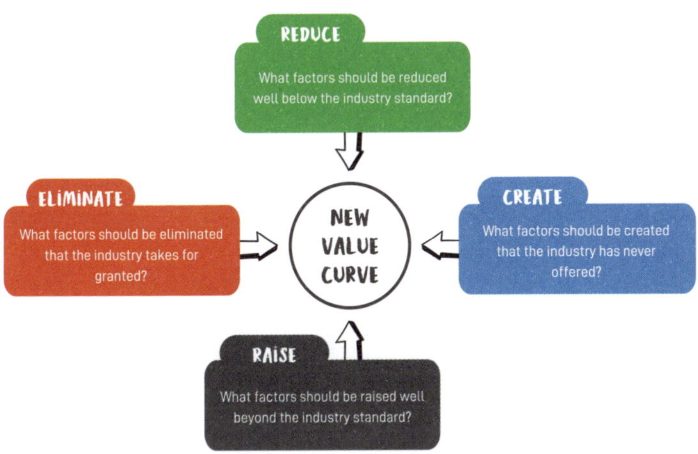

What are the best practices for a business expansion programme?

In order to expand a business it is necessary to know the answers to several questions. Those questions can be grouped into a set of best practices.

Business expansion best practices
Who is our client? Is this the ideal client? Who would the ideal client be? How can we mainly serve our ideal clients?
What is our value proposition? Is it unique? How did we get to this value proposition? What is there that makes it different from the existing value propositions? What is there for our clients that they cannot get anywhere? Are these our strengths? Is this being clearly communicated?
What are our competitors offering? Where are they operating? In the same industry, or not?
What are the vacant spaces in the market that prospective competitors may exploit? What are they doing well? And not so well?
What business indicators are we using? What key indicators are we using to assess the need for expansion? What alternatives are there for these indicators? Are our revenue streams and what can we do differently to improve them? How sustainable are they? What other products are we selling whose results are not good, and how important is it that we keep them?
What is supporting our strengths and helping us recognize opportunities? What kind of resources? How dependent are we on them? How stimulated are these? What is the revenue stream that we can obtain from them in the future?

KEY IDEAS AND REFERENCES FOR MORE INFORMATION

- Competitors are the first step in thinking about a strategic programme for a business
- The option of developing a blue ocean instead of navigating in a red ocean is critical for strategic growth
- Value creation is the essence of a strategic programme

[1] Porter, M. E. (1985). Competitive Advantage: Creating and Sustaining Superior Performance. New York.

[2] Porter, M. E. (2008). On Competition, Updated and Expanded Edition Hardcover. Howard Business School Press, Boston.

[3] Kim, W. C., & Mauborgne, R. A. (2014). Blue ocean strategy, expanded edition: How to create uncontested market space and make the competition irrelevant. Harvard Business Review Press.

[4] Kim, W. C., & Mauborgne, R. (2017). Blue ocean shift: Beyond competing-proven steps to inspire confidence and seize new growth. Hachette UK.

4

How to find, deal with and manage investors?

How to find investors?

There is no magic way to raise money for a business. The possible options depend on many factors and the most relevant ones relate to three questions:

What is the business plan/business case?	**Who** is looking for the investors?	**What** is the investor profile required?

Regarding the first question, see Vol. 1 of the BCR. Subsequently, we will consider the other two questions:

Why is it important to know who is looking for investors?

The profiles of the leaders of the team seeking the investment are critical, because of their important role in generating the trust of investors. Both direct credibility (investors' first impressions) and indirect credibility (which results from the 'quality' of the information provided during the investor's approach made) are important factors. We never get a second chance to make a good first impression. In addition, it is often not possible to chase the same investors a second time, following an unsuccessful first approach. Credibility is a very important asset and this is why it is very often advisable to use consultants for this fundamental step. Unfortunately, it is not uncommon to see entrepreneurs approaching investors, without having rigorously prepared their approach.

What are investor profiles for business?

There are several types of investor, and they can be classified based on many different criteria, relating to risk (higher or lower profile), time (short to long), the degree of maturity of the investments (startups to established business), the scale of investment, or even the topics under analysis (more technology-based or more finance-based, for instance). These characteristics can be grouped into three definitions, corresponding to the previous factors:

1. The Conservative

The conservative investor prioritises security and liquidity much more than profitability. Thus, the conservative has zero tolerance for losses and risks, which naturally leads him or her to give up on the larger return that comes with higher-risk investments. The investor with this profile likes to have their investments deposited in applications without much volatility so that he or she can leave them there and rest. This does not mean that he or she does not monitor them, but rather that there is no reason for very strong "emotions" like the ones that can occur in the stock market, for example. In the case of riskier applications, the conservative profile appreciates rescue power, or immediate liquidity, and would not be able to tolerate 15 or 30 days waiting while watching their precious investments declining. This profile is in search of, or comfortable with, short to medium term investments ranging from 0- 5 years. Usually, new investors who are just getting started will easily fit this profile. Over time, after acquiring more experience, their profile may change.

> Typical investment Portfolio: At least 80% applied to Fixed Income and little or nothing in Variable Income.

2. The Moderate

The moderate investor has one foot in the Conservative and the other in the Aggressive profile, making it safe to say that this is a more balanced profile. This profile has greater tolerance for risks than the conservative but not as much as the aggressive; it is willing to give up a little more on liquidity and security to obtain the desired returns. This profile is in search of, or comfortable with, medium to long term investments from 5 to 10 years.

> Typical investment Portfolio: 60–65% applied to Fixed Income and the rest in Variable Income and Funds

3. The Aggressive

The aggressive investor prioritises profitability above all factors and has great tolerance for risks. This is usually a savvy investor with more money, and so he or she is willing to give up on immediate liquidity tending to be more flexible with greater tolerance for losses because he or she understands that higher profits will come in the long run. This profile is in search of, or comfortable with, long term investments of 10+ years.

> Typical investment Portfolio: More than 50% applied to Variable Income.

Source: adapted from https://blog.goodaudience.com/3-basic-risk-investor-profiles-73e796bebb2f, consulted in 23/8/2019.

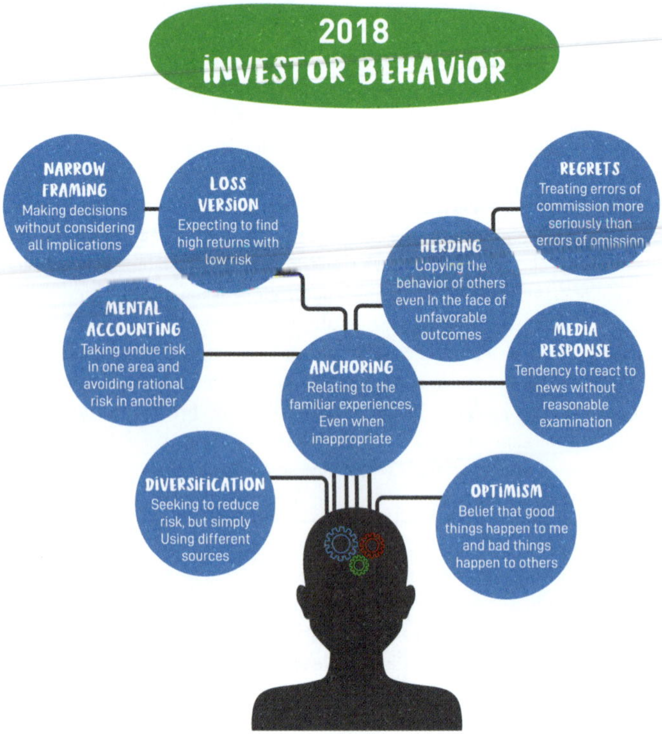

Source: adapted from www.dalbar.com, accessed 20 June 2019.

Why is it important to understand what investors are looking for?

To manage the relationship with investors is critical to understand what they are interested in. By knowing what drives the investor's approach, it is possible to know which investors to target and to prepare appropriate communication strategies.

As a rule of thumb, investors tend to look for the so-called "4 M's," depending on their profile.

Momentum	1. Momentum for the Business Idea. Everyone has their own definition of momentum. Basically the momentum refers to the feeling that there is a combination of factors available in a window of opportunity.
Management	2. Management Team. This is really a sine qua non condition for investors. Few investors believe that the team can be set after other decisions are made. In fact, it is difficult to start with a good product/service idea and business model, and get the best team only afterwards. This may be possible but is less likely to occur than a situation in which the team is known from the very beginning.
Market	3. Market potential. If there is not a clear and demonstrated idea about the market potential for a business idea, it will be extremely difficult to convince any investor.
Money	4. Money. At the end of the day, investors will be interested in the profit and loss of the business. Potential business performance is, therefore, the bottom line.

How should the relationships with different types of investors be managed?

It is critical to consider investors as a special type of internal client. Thus, it is necessary to have a special focus and mindset directed towards fulfilling the investor's expectation. As with any client, it is critical to understand (1) what he or she needs; (2) what he or she says that he or she wants; (3) what he or she really wants.

At this level, it is crucial to be able to read between the lines. Managing relationships properly requires making a psychological profile of all the people involved, as well as related stakeholders. Thus, the profile required here goes beyond the 'business profile'. The specific framework and inter-relationships between the links with the investor and other stakeholders always provides added value in the management of the relationships.

What is the role of mediation in managing investors?

Mediation is often confused with consulting, mentoring or coaching but is in fact a very different process - whether in business or in other fields. Mediation involves the connection between three or more parties, and requires a 'hands-on', invasive approach. The mediator is typical a neutral party who acts between two or more parties that require help to find and agree on their common interests.

Mediation can be very important not only in avoiding problems but also in finding the appropriate solutions. An external view can provide help to avoid bottlenecks. The mediation may involve several tasks, from consulting, to coaching and mentoring.

For its part, consulting is a process where two parties interact so that one of them - the consultant - provides new information to the other (the client or beneficiary). Coaching provides a process in which this information is put into practice by the client. Mentoring is most often defined as a professional relationship in which an experienced person (the mentor) assists another (the mentoree) in developing specific skills and knowledge that will enhance the less-experienced person's professional and personal growth.

KEY IDEAS AND REFERENCES FOR MORE INFORMATION

- The business case is a mandatory tool when looking for investors
- The choice of the investor profile is a critical factor that guarantees the fit among the two parts involved in the mediation
- The business profile of the investor should be complemented by the psychological profile of the persons involved
- Mediation is often a critical factor for a smooth investor management

[1] Rappaport, A. (1997) Creating Shareholder Value: A Guide for Managers and Investors. Simon and Schuster.
[2] Pape, S. (2007) The Barefoot Investor: Five Steps to Financial Freedom. Pluto Press Australia.
[3] Leadbeater, C., & Leadbeater, C. (2000). Living on thin air: The new economy. London: Penguin.

5

What are the best practices for raising money for a developing business?

What is the best way to raise money for a developing business?

There are many options for raising money for a business. The options depend on many factors and the most relevant can be described as 'the business framework' or the business context. Often it is relevant to combine different options along the process and evolution of a business, namely:

Type of business or sector	The stage and scale of the business	Geographic or stakeholder constraints

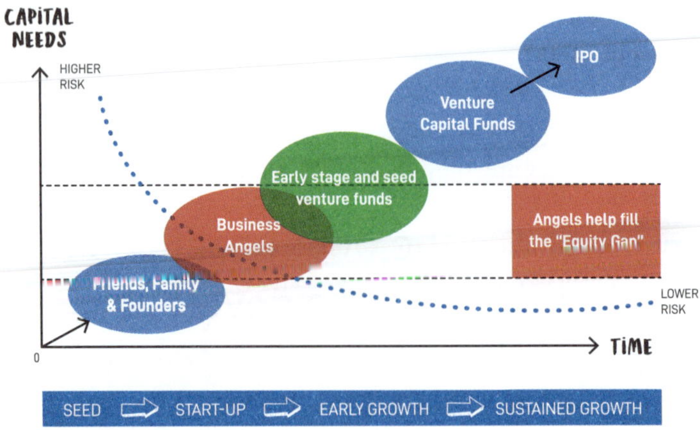

Source: Prieto (2015). "Business Angel investing across Europe", EBAN – The European Trade Association for Business Angels, Seed Funds and Early Stage Market Players.

What are the different types of financing opportunities?

There are three major types of financing opportunities for business, depending on the flow of financial assets.

Grants and donations	Loans	Investments
Non-refundable	Interest rate involved	Return on investment margin involved
Self-funding Family and friends Crowdfunding Business contests and prizes Government or institutional incentives	Microfinance Credit card based financing Conventional banks Crowdfunding based loans Financing in the value chain (*)	Business angels Venture capital Equity investment Corporate venturing
(*) not exactly a direct loan but, conceptually, a loan process.		

What are grants and donations, as financing opportunities?

In most cases, grants and donations are not refundable, and even when they are, they do not have an interest rate associated.

Self-funding, also known as bootstrapping, is an effective method of startup financing, especially when a business is just starting. First-time entrepreneurs often have trouble getting funding without first showing some traction and a plan for potential success. Entrepreneurs can invest from their own savings. This is an easy way to raise financing, because there are fewer formalities/compliance requirements, and less cost involved. Self-funding or bootstrapping should be considered as a first funding option because of its advantages. When entrepreneurs use their own money, they are tied to the business. Later on, investors consider it a good sign if entrepreneurs have used their own savings - because it shows that they believed in what they were doing.

This is suitable only if the initial requirement is small. Some businesses need money right from day one, and for such businesses, bootstrapping may not be a good option.

Friends and Family Loans. Friends and family have a personal vested interest in watching the entrepreneur succeed. This might make them more willing to invest in the business, especially at the beginning. In most situations, family and friends are flexible when it comes to the interest rate. Taking money from friends and family, however, can be tricky, and all the pros and cons should be scrutinised before deciding to use this method to generate funds.

Raise Funds by Winning Contests. Contests encourage entrepreneurs with business ideas to set up their own businesses. In such competitions, entrepreneurs have either to build a product or prepare a business plan. Winning these competitions can also attract some media coverage. The business case should be comprehensive enough to convince anyone that the idea is worth investing in. There are organisations that offer monetary rewards - or even financing - for businesses and entrepreneurs who enter their contests. Eligibility requirements, entry fees and judging criteria vary widely. Several municipalities/local councils offer these incentives in order to attract and keep young entrepreneurs in their region. An increase in the number of contests has helped tremendously in maximising opportunities for fund raising.

Government Loans for startup or developing business. Most governments (at national or regional levels) have a vested interest in the continued growth and success of the small business sector. As a result, different government bodies offer many different types of loan to help entrepreneurs to get started. Several businesses started this way.

Crowdfunding is a newer way of funding a startup that has gained a lot of popularity in recent years. Crowdfunding is like taking a loan, pre-order, contribution or investment from more than one person at the same time. These people can be located all over the world. An entrepreneur will place a detailed description of his/her business on a crowdfunding platform. He/she will outline the goals of the business, plans for making profit, how much funding is necessary and for what reasons, and so on. Then consumers can read about the business and give money if they like the idea. Those giving money will make online pledges, with the promise of pre-buying the product or giving a donation. Anyone can contribute towards helping a business whose aims they really believe in. The best thing about crowdfunding is that it can also generate interest and hence help in marketing the product as well as financing it, even before the product is launched. It also has the advantage of helping the entrepreneur gauge whether there is demand for the product. In other words, it can work as a pre-pre-test. This process can cut out professional investors and brokers by putting funding in the hands of the general public. It also might attract venture-capital investment down the line if a company has a particularly successful campaign. Examples of crowdfunding platforms include: www.kickstarter.com, www.indiegogo.com, www.gofundme.com, www.crowdfunder.co.uk, www.ppl.pt and www.rockethub.pt.

What are the different types of business loans?

Money through Bank Loans. Banks tend to be the first port of call for entrepreneurs who are thinking about funding. The bank provides two kinds of financing for businesses: working capital loan, and funding. Working capital loan is the loan required to run one complete cycle of revenue-generating operations. The limit is usually decided by hypothecating stocks and debtors. Funding from a bank involves the usual process of sharing the business plan and the valuation details assumed for the business, along with the project report, based on which the loan is sanctioned.

Microfinance. Microfinance is basically access to financial services for those who do not have access to conventional banking services. Increasingly, it is becoming popular for those whose requirements are limited and whose credit ratings are not favoured by banks. Most organisations have maximum values that are under €30,000. Most commonly used by non-profit organizations, microloans are granted by institutions to individuals who do not normally qualify for a traditional bank loan. Instead of gifting a donation to the non-profit organisation, microloan organisations allow individuals to invest in economic opportunities. Microloans are very popular in small and developing nations as well. They typically cover values below €10,000.

Credit Cards: Business credit cards are among the most readily available ways to finance a startup and can be a quick way to get instant money. However, one should bear in mind that interest rates and costs on the cards can grow very quickly, and carrying that debt can be detrimental to a business owner's credit.

Funding From Business Incubators and Accelerators. Early stage businesses can consider Incubator and Accelerator programs as funding options. These programs assist hundreds of startup businesses every year. Though used interchangeably, there are few fundamental differences between the two terms. Incubators are like a parent to a child, nurturing the business, providing shelter, tools, training and network. Accelerators share some similarities, but while an incubator helps/nurtures a business taking its first steps, an accelerator helps it to run/develop/take a giant leap.

Crowdfunding loans. Depending on the crowdfunding platform there are two types: (1) the best known is small funds in the form of donations or an exchange of money for the promise of a product sample; (2) less well-known is the possibility of getting loans from platforms that are (at the time of writing) typically lower than €20,000; some good examples are: www.mintos.com, www.crowdfunding-platforms.com and www.raize.pt.

What is value chain finance?

Purchase order financing option. Many different factors can affect the cash flow of a business, including seasonality and supply and demand. For example, some companies may find themselves unable to fulfil a large order due to a lack of funds to purchase the materials needed to produce the goods. In these instances, purchase order financing might be the answer. A purchase order-financing organisation will essentially extend an advance so the organisation can purchase the materials it needs immediately and then recoup the money once the goods are sold. Companies that most often qualify for purchase order financing are those that deal in manufactured goods - not services - and that stand to make a margin of 20% or more on the sale. A good example of a firm that has used this type of financing is Tesla.

Financing by suppliers or vendors. If your ability to pay your bills is contingent on your ability to sell your product, you may benefit from negotiating longer payment terms with your vendors. Most vendors require payment on invoices within 30 days, before implementing late fees and penalties. You may be able to negotiate a longer term that gives you more cash to work with in the interim. This is especially important if you have a sales cycle longer than 30 days. If it takes 45 days from purchase of goods to sale, you will never be able to pay your invoices in 30 days. This takes negotiation and may not be an option for all vendors.

Product pre-sale financing. Selling products before they are launched is an often-overlooked and highly effective way to raise the money needed for financing a business. This approach consists of accepting orders with a partial pre-payment. This is a great way to improve cash flow and prepare for consumer demand. If the business is based purely on the selling of a single product, the easiest way to raise the money to produce the product may be to pre-sell it. This option also provides a good indication of the business potential.

How to get financial investors?

Angel investors are individuals with surplus cash and a keen interest to invest in upcoming startups. They also work in groups of networks to collectively screen proposals before investing. They can also offer mentoring or advice alongside capital. Angel Investment as a funding option has its shortcomings too. This alternative form of investing generally occurs during a company's early stages of growth, with investors expecting up to 30% equity. Angel investors invest lesser amounts than venture capitalists. Typically, business angels in Europe invest in multiples of €50,000.

Venture capitals are professionally managed funds, which invest in companies that have significant potential. They usually invest in a business against equity and exit when there is an IPO or an acquisition. Venture capitals provide expertise, mentorship and act as an acid test of where the organisation is going, evaluating the business from the sustainability and scalability point of view. A venture capital investment may be appropriate for small businesses that are beyond the startup phase, but that are already generating revenues.

Private equity provides long-term, committed share capital, to help unquoted companies to grow and to succeed. When looking to start up, to expand, to buy a business, to buy a division of a parent company, to turnaround or to revitalise a company, private equity can help. Obtaining private equity is very different from raising debt or a loan from a lender, such as a bank. While lenders have a legal right to interest on a loan and to the repayment of the capital, irrespective of your success or failure, private equity does not. In fact, private equity is invested in exchange for a stake in the company and, as shareholders, the investors' returns are dependent on the growth and profitability of the business.

What is corporate venturing?

Corporate venturing has developed rapidly in recent years. However, it still represents a small fraction of investment when compared to private equity investment. Direct corporate venturing occurs when a corporation takes a direct minority stake in an unquoted company or business-developing project. This is usually done by large companies who wish to invest in small but innovative startup firms. Corporate venturers raise their funds from their parent organisations and/or from external sources. The investing company may also provide the startup with management and marketing expertise, strategic direction, and/or a line of credit. Sometimes the business ventures are originated inside the corporate venture initiator. In this case, the capital searches for business to invest in.

KEY IDEAS AND REFERENCES FOR MORE INFORMATION

- There are many options for the financing of business activities and that depends on the framework (How much? What for? When?)
- It is possible to combine different financing tools but some of them can interfere with others
- Knowledge about the financing options allows the companies to rank the different options
- When following the loan to investor path it is good practice to have appropriate advice

[1] Rose, N. (2016) Equity Crowdfunding: The Complete Guide For Startups And Growing Companies. Stonepine Publishing.

[2] Miller, D. and Pugh, N. (2018), Six Figure Crowdfunding: The No Bullsh*t Guide to Running a Life-Changing Campaign, BOOM! Studios.

[3] Thiel, P. and Masters, B. (2014) Zero to One: Notes on Startups, or How to Build the Future. Broadway Business, Currency.

[4] Mazzucato, M. (2015) The Entrepreneurial State: Debunking Public vs. Private Sector Myths (vol. 1). Anthem Press.

6

How are investment rounds organised and how to use them?

What is the financing cycle?

The financing cycle is the set of possible options that are sequentially possible for different businesses. Understanding these options is critical for the growth and expansion of new or existing business. Each investment round will require a business case or a business plan, depending on the specific stakeholders.

The terms that most private equity firms use to define the stage of a company's development are determined by the purpose for which the financing is required.

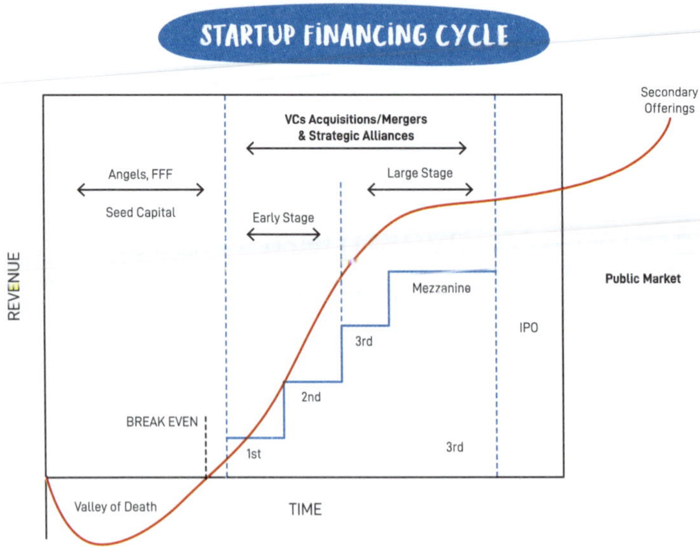

What is a Seed investment?

Seed investment is necessary to allow a business concept to be developed, possibly involving the production of a business plan, prototypes and additional research. This happens prior to bringing a product to market and commencing large-scale manufacturing. Only a few seed financings are undertaken each year by private equity firms. Many seed financings are too small and require too much hands-on support from the private equity firm to make them economically viable as investments. There are, however, some specialist private equity firms, who may be worth approaching, subject to the company meeting their other investment preferences. Business angel capital should also be considered, as having a business angel on a company's board may be more attractive to private equity firms when later stage funds are required.

What is Start-up investment?

Start-up investment is necessary to develop the company's products and fund their initial marketing. Companies may be in the process of being set up or may have been trading for a short time, but not have sold their product commercially.

Although many start-ups are typically smaller companies, there is an increasing number of multi-million euro start-ups. Several private equity and venture capitalists will consider high quality and generally larger start-up propositions as well as investing in the later stages. However, there are those who specialise in the start-up stage, subject to the company seeking investment meeting the firm's other investment preferences.

What are other early stage investment possibilities?

Early stage investment is necessary to initiate commercial manufacturing and sales, namely in companies that have completed the product development stage, but may not yet be generating profits.

This is a stage that has been attracting an increasing amount of private equity over the past few years.

SEED, SERIES A, B, C FUNDING

FAMILY AND FRIENDS ROUND
An easy and fast way of raising initial funds in exchange for equity to family and friends.

SEED ROUND
A seed round is often used to inject capital to cover expenses and build traction until a startup can start earning revenue.

SERIES A
The first round of shares offered to external investors during early-stage investment. Startups are likely to have a product and user base.

SERIES B
The second stage is focused on continuing to scale the company. It is likely that its business model has been established and there is traction with customers.

SERIES C ONWARDS
Subsequent venture rounds are used to scale the company, make acquisitions, maximise market share, grow internationally and prepare the company for an acquisition or public listing.

Source: https://medium.com/@edc.iitghy/fundraising-everything-you-need-to-know-e946e4343d4a, consulted in 23/8/2019.

What is series A, B, C or D or expansion investment?

This terminology refers to different stages of expansion, with increasing levels of investment and historical data at each stage. To grow and expand an established company usually involves following a sequential series of investments - for example, financing increased production capacity, product development and marketing, and to provide additional working capital. This type of investment is also known as "development" or "growth" capital.

What kind of financial operation are usually developed?

There is a set of complex operations that can be developed depending on the business context and requirements. It is very important to know and understand the terminology to be able to explore specific opportunities in greater depth. Appropriate consulting and mediation is usually required.

Management buy-out (MBO) enables the current operating management and investors to acquire or to purchase a significant shareholding in the product line or business they manage. MBOs range from the acquisition of relatively small formerly family-owned businesses to buyouts well in excess of 100 million euros. The amounts concerned tend to be larger than with other types of financing, as they involve the acquisition of an entire business.

Management buy-in (MBI) enables a manager (or group of managers) from outside a company to buy into it.

Buy-in management buy-out (BIMBO) enables a company's management to acquire the business they manage with the assistance of some incoming management.

Institutional buy-out (IBO) enables a private equity firm to acquire a company, following which the incumbent and/or incoming management will be given or acquire a stake in the business.

This is a relatively new term and is an increasingly used method of buy-out. It is a method, which is often preferred by vendors, as it reduces the number of parties with whom they have to negotiate.

Secondary purchase. This is when a private equity firm acquires existing shares in a company from another private equity firm or from another shareholder or shareholders.

Replacement equity. This allows existing non-private equity investors to buy back or redeem part, or all, of another investor's shareholding.

Rescue/turnaround involves financing a company in difficulty, or rescuing it from receivership. It may include a refinancing bank debt and the reduction of a company's level of gearing.

Bridge financing. Short-term private equity funding is provided to a company generally planning to float within a year.

Investment banks organise the provision of medium to longer-term loans, usually for larger amounts than clearing banks. Later they can play an important role in the process of "going public" by advising on the terms and price of public issues and by arranging underwriting when necessary.

Finance houses provide various forms of instalment credit, ranging from hire purchase to leasing. This is often asset-based, and usually for a fixed term and at fixed interest rates.

Factoring companies provide finance by buying trade debts at a discount, either on a recourse basis (you retain the credit risk on the debts) or on a non-recourse basis (the factoring company takes over the credit risk).

Mezzanine finance is loan finance that is halfway between equity and secured debt. These facilities either require a second charge on the company's assets or are unsecured. Because the risk is consequently higher than with senior debt, the interest charged by the mezzanine debt provider will be higher than that from the principal lenders and sometimes a modest equity "up-side" will be required through options or warrants. It is generally most appropriate for larger transactions.

Government and European Commission sources provide financial aid to companies, ranging from project grants (related to jobs created and safeguarded) to enterprise loans in selected areas – see above.

The private equity investment process

Stage	Entrepreneur	Entrepreneurs (s) and Equity firm	Private Equity company	Reports
Approaching the Private Equity firm / evaluating the Business Plan	• Appoint advisers • Prepare Business Plan • Contact Equity firm		• Review business plan	**Business plan**
⇓				
Initial enquires and negotiation	• Provide additional info	• Meet to discuss the business plan • Build relationships • Negotiate outline terms	• Conduct initial enquires • Value the business • Consider financing structure	**Offer letter**
⇓				
Due diligence		• Liaise with accountants • Liaise with other external consultants	• Initiate external due diligence	**Consultant reports** **Accountants reports**
⇓				
Final negotiation and completion	• Disclose all relevant business information	• Negotiate final terms • Document constitution and voting rights	• Draw up completion documentation	**Disclosures** **Warranties** **Memorandum** **Shareholders agreement**
⇓				
Monitoring	• Provide periodic management accounts • Communicate regularly with investors		• Seat on board? • Monitor investment • Constructive input • Involvement in major decisions	**Management accounts** **Minutes of board and other key meetings**
⇓				
EXIT				

Source: adapted from: www.bvca.co.uk, accessed in 20/6/2019.

For recent information regarding the actual amounts invested at each stage of investment, see the "BVCA Report on Investment Activity", available at: http://www.bvca.co.uk/Research.

What is the main difficulty for entrepreneurs in the financing process?

The main challenge facing business founders in the financing process is the dilution of capital along different investment rounds. How to address this dilution is a problem that firms often have to face. There are several ways to cope with the dilution process: (1) being able to value intangible assets and incorporate them in the capital of the company; (2) establishing a corporate share structure with different share powers including golden shares; (3) defining contract-based processes that protect minority investors or investors in early investment rounds.

When intellectual property and other intangible assets are at stake, the frameworks to be used might be very complex. Therefore, it is mandatory to consult specialised lawyers at this stage, since the specific conditions may vary greatly.

KEY IDEAS AND REFERENCES FOR MORE INFORMATION

- Financing is usually the fuel that makes businesses grow
- Depending on the evolution stage of the company, different financing options might be appropriate
- The complexity of financing for growth can be very high and require the involvement of specialists

[1] Hudson, M. (2014) Funds: Private Equity, Hedge and All Core Structures. John Wiley & Sons.

[2] Arundale, K. (2010) Guide to Private Equity. British Private Equity & Venture Capital Association. Available at https://www.bvca.co.uk/Portals/0/library/Files/Website%20files/2012_0001_guide_to_private_equity.pdf

[3] Nijs, L. (2013) Mezzanine Financing: Tools, Applications and Total Performance. John Wilwy & Sons.

[4] Francisco, R. A. (2012) Finance for Academics: A Guide to Investment for Income. Springer Science & Business Media.

7

What is the evolution process from startup, scaleup and scaler?

What is the business evolution process for technology companies?

Technology companies, either product- or service-based, evolve throughout their financing process. At the present time there are no established definitions globally agreed for the evolution normally associated with startups. The concept is often understood differently in Europe than it is in the US. Other countries will tend to follow either European or US logic, depending on which region they are in.

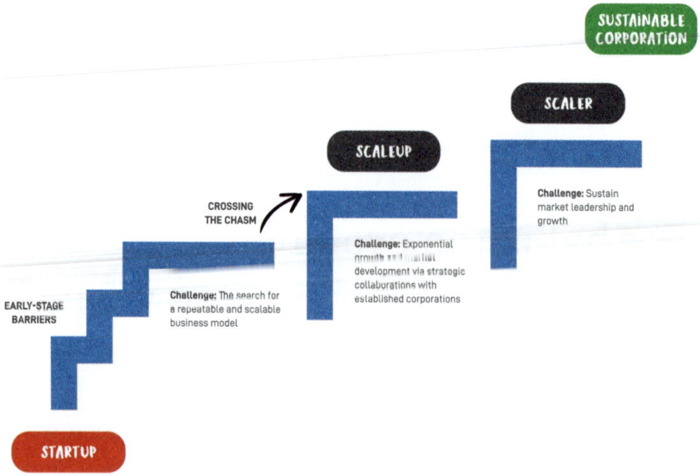

Source: adapted from: https://startupeuropepartnership.eu, and from Moore, G. A., & McKenna, R. (1999). Crossing the Chasm: Marketing and Selling Disruptive Products to Mainstream Customers, Harper Collins. accessed in 20/6/2019.

What is a startup company?

A startup company (or start-up) is an entrepreneurial venture, which is typically a newly-emerged, fast-growing business. The definition of the startup usually refers to a company, a partnership or an organisation designed to develop rapidly a scalable business model. These companies are generally involved in the design and implementation of the innovative processes of development, validation and research for target markets. The term became internationally widespread during the dot-com bubble, when a great many dot-com companies were founded.

The origins of the term "startup" can be traced back as being cited in the Oxford English Dictionary (1989 edition). In the business sense, the term was first recorded in 1976 Forbes (15 Aug. edition: 6): "*The unfashionable business of investing in startups in the electronic data processing field*". The Start-up company arrived a year later; in 1977, Business Week (5 Sept. edition) made reference to it as an incubator for startup companies, especially in the fast-growth, high-technology field.

A startup is a registered business entity. Any unregistered entity is just a work in progress, or simply an idea. A startup has an organisational structure (no matter how horizontal it may be), has employees on the payroll, and has shares divided among shareholders. It tends to exploit a market niche with great potential, although is also limited as regards time. Startups are typically born from innovative business ideas, but, unlike spinoffs, they are not usually created inside another organisation. They have typically fewer than a hundred employees, have been established for under five years and have a turnover of less than 50 million (either € or US$).

When is a startup no longer a startup?

Startup means growth. Growth seems to be a differentiator for many people when trying to define a startup. According to Paul Graham, founder of Y Combinator: "*A startup is a company designed to grow fast.*". A startup is focused on growth, and to have the potential for significant growth, a company must "*(a) make something lots of people want, and (b) reach and serve all those people.*" That is why Graham does not count, say, a florist or other local business as a startup.

Typically, businesses should no longer be called startups when they achieve a certain scale:
5+ years in business — a company has spent at least five years pursuing the same customers and market.
1,000+ paying customers — a company has found people who are willing to pay for their solution. (For some companies selling solutions at a very high price, it might take only 100 customers to prove that there is real value in the offering.)
100+ teammates - a company has a sizeable team that covers most of the core functions that a high-growth organisation needs in order to scale.

Conceptually, the company shifts from growth optimisation to optimising for something else; it stops being a startup and becomes a scaleup.

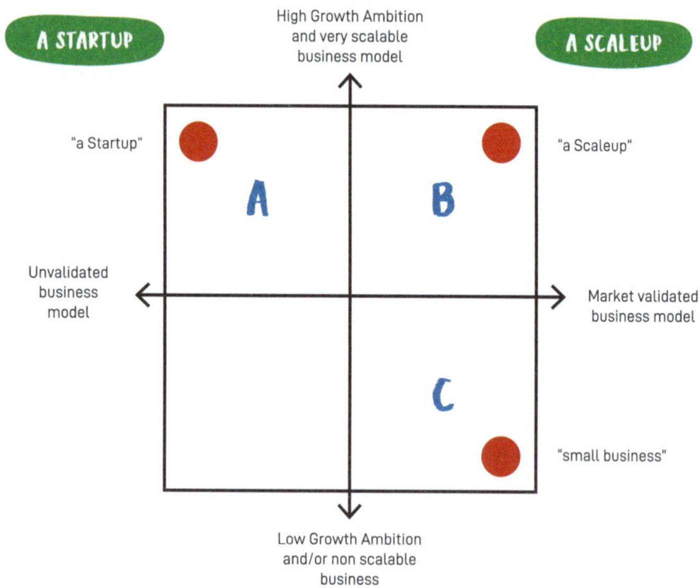

Source: https://www.startupcommons.org/what-is-a-startup.html, consulted in 23/8/2019.

What is a scaleup company?

A **scaleup** company is a business looking to grow and expand (startups with >$1M funding raised since foundation and at least one funding round in the last 5-year period) in terms of market access, revenues, added value or number of employees - in particular, identifying and realising win-win opportunities for collaboration between market leaders and market disruptors. Scaleups are often considered the next wave of innovation and are credited as the collaborative road to sustainable growth.

Scaleups still lack a clear definition. When does your startup become a scaleup? A scaleup is defined as being a development-stage business, specific to high-technology markets, that is looking to grow in terms of market access, revenues, and number of employees, adding value by identifying and realising win-win opportunities for collaboration with established companies. As with any capital-intensive company, the financing goal for a scaleup is to reward its investors, either by being acquired via an M&A or an IPO.

What is a scaler company?

A scaler company is considered to be a business that is able to raise over >$100 M. The term has become more popular due to the acknowledgement of the emerging trend by various organisations and people.

What are Spin-Off, Split-Off and Carve-Out companies?

There is specific terminology relating to the process of how companies can be created:

Spinoffs	There are several 'definitions' of Spinoffs, Spin-offs or Spin Offs, but there is a global agreement that the creation of a spinoff takes place within another organisation, which can be a firm, an academic institution or a research institute. A spinoff is therefore the creation of an independent company through the sale or distribution of new shares of an existing business or division of a parent organisation. Most spin-offs tend to perform better than the overall market and, in some cases, better than their parent companies.
	There are different methods a company can use to divest certain assets, a division, or a subsidiary. Corporate spin-offs happen when the parent company distributes shares of the subsidiary that is being spun-off to its existing shareholders on a pro rata basis, in the form of a special dividend. The parent company typically receives no cash consideration for the spin-off. Existing shareholders benefit by now holding shares of two separate companies after the spin-off instead of one. The spin-off is a distinct entity from the parent company and has its own management. The parent company may spin off 100% of the shares in its subsidiary, or it may spin off 80% to its shareholders and hold a minority interest of less than 20% in the subsidiary.
	Spinout happens when a corporate spin-off starbursts. It is a type of corporate action where a company also "splits off" a section as a completely separate business without ties to the parent organisation.
Split-off	In a split-off, shareholders in the parent company are offered shares in a subsidiary, but the catch is they have to choose between holding shares of the subsidiary or the parent company.
Carve-out	In a carve-out, the parent company sells some or all of the shares in its subsidiary to the public through an initial public offering (IPO). Unlike a spin-off, the parent company generally receives a cash inflow through a carve-out. Since shares are sold to the public, a carve-out also establishes a net set of shareholders in the subsidiary. A carve-out often precedes the full spin-off of the subsidiary to the parent company's shareholders.

Source: adapted from Joe Cornell Bloomberg Spin-Off Conference 2016.

What are the business size metrics, as defined by the European Commission?

The terminology currently used in Europe follows recommendations by the European Commission defined in 2003, and amended in 2006. The framework references and constraints must refer to official documents from the Commission. The key information can be summarised as follows:

Enterprise category	Headcount annual workout unit	Annual turnover		Annual balance sheet total
Medium-sized	< 250	≤ 50 M€	or	≤ 45 M€
Small	< 50	≤ 10 M€		≤ 10 M€
Micro	< 10	≤ 2 M€		≤ 2 M€

Source: adapted from https://ec.europa.eu/eurostat/web/structural-business-statistics/structural-business-statistics/sme, consulted in 23/8/2019 - Definition of Small Medium size Enterprises Source: EUROPEAN COMMISSION, Commission Recommendation of 6 May 2003 concerning the definition of micro, small and medium-sized enterprises 1 1 Commission recommendation of 6 may (2003) concerning the definition of micro, small and medium-sized enterprises, Official journal of the European union-L124/36

KEY IDEAS AND REFERENCES FOR MORE INFORMATION

- Business scale and the evolution process leads to the terminology of startups, scaleups and scallers
- Business origin and corporate financing or links leads to the terminology of Spinoffs, Spinouts, Splitoffs or Carveout companies
- Business scale, turnover and number of employees leads to the European terminology of Micro, Small and Large companies
- The complexity of financing options requires studying and evaluating them in detail

[1] Ries, E. (2011) The Lean Startup: How Today's Entrepreneurs Use Continuous Innovation to Create Radically Successful Business. Crown Business, New York.

[2] Moore, G. A. (1991) Crossing the Chasm, Marketing and Selling High-tech Products to Mainstream Customers. Harper Business, NY.

[3] Rose, D.S. (2016) The Startup Checklist: 25 Steps to a Scalable, High-Growth Business. John Wiley & Sons.

[4] Cremades, A. (2016) The Art of Startup Fundraising: Pitching Investors, Negotiating the Deal, and Everything Else Entrepreneurs Need to Know. John Wiley & Sons.

[5] Moore, G. A. (2015) Zone to Win: Organizing to Compete in an Age of Disruption. Diversion Books.

[6] Yu, H. (2018) Leap: How to Thrive in a World Where Everything Can Be Copied. Hachette, UK.

[7] Harnish, V. (2014) Scaling Up: How a Few Companies Make It...and Why the Rest Don't. Gazelles. Inc.

8

Why do some companies grow faster?

What is business growth?

Business growth is the result of a process where organisations become larger, in either valuation, turnover, number of clients and/or number of employees. Like a living organism, a business organisation is directed towards growth. Growth is a natural process in business. However, at a certain tipping point, the organisation stops growing and eventually needs to be re-invented, shrinks and dies, or divides into smaller organisations or is acquired by or merged with another one.

What are the best practices to promote business growth?

There are no established best practices for business growth because much depends on the sector of activity, the type of leadership and the geographical context. The framework or starting point is very important when looking for good practices. However, it is possible to evaluate the recommendations of several entrepreneurs for practices that promote healthy growth.

Relevant factors for companies aiming at growing, according to top managers
Company's Culture "With each new addition to your team, the camaraderie and company culture will inevitably change. It is important to not overlook your company culture but instead have a plan to foster and develop the initial spirit as the numbers grow. Your culture is what brought them to the company in the first place, so it is imperative not to lose it!" Kim Kaupe, ZinePak
Knowledge Management "A small company often captures its working knowledge in the minds of its early employees. As a result, you may struggle to educate new hires, and some people may have a disproportionate amount of power or responsibility simply because of what they know (rather than what they can do). To grow smoothly, be disciplined about documenting your best practices and sharing them with your team." AJ Shankar, Everlaw, Inc.
Clearly Defined Roles "It's imperative to clearly define each person's role in the company, especially when you start to grow. This includes the founding team and those first hires. Take the time to clearly define roles, responsibility and a chain of command so everyone is on the same page." Andrew Thomas, SkyBell Video Doorbell
Continued Scalability "We recently updated a number of our processes and the structures within our company simply because a lot of what we had in place works today, but would not be appropriate or even feasible with four times the number of employees. For instance, we found that how we all share stories about the weekend in a roundtable format would not work when 30 people were at the table." Beck Bamberger, BAM Communications
Each Small Step "As entrepreneurs, we like to explore, we're curious and we always get involved in new projects. This is good. But it's easy to forget to create processes to establish stability and consistency. You should keep in mind your vision and determine the steps you need to take to get from where you are to where you want to be." Alfredo Atanacio, Uassist.ME
Cash Flow "Don't overlook how much money is coming in, and balance it with the money you are spending to grow. As Warren Buffet says: "Cash or available credit is like oxygen: you don't notice it 99.9 percent of the time, but when absent, it's the only thing you notice." Kevin Henrikson, Acompli (now Outlook iOS/Android @ Microsoft)

Development of Internal Tools
"When the company is small, a lot of tasks are done manually as it's not worthwhile to build a custom tool or buy a product to service the need. As the business grows, a lot of processes inside the company have to be assessed and optimized by building internal tools to streamline operations."
Randy Rayess, VenturePact

Consistent Team Quality
"Even if you are generating significant cash flow or have just landed a new investment and want to grow your team, you should never settle. Your team is always as weak as the weakest link. You must always keep the quality of your team as high as possible."
Luke Skurman, Niche.com

Customer Happiness
"As your company grows and you bring on more new business, it's important to remain steadfast in your focus on existing customer happiness. We monitor this through tracking net promoter score and customer retention. This metric gives us a good indicator of whether the business is scaling appropriately and is likely to see increased total business."
Ryan Wilson, FiveFifty

Core Values
"Maintaining values and culture is crucial to long-term sustainability and growth, and a strong argument can be made that these two areas indirectly impact profitability. Having core values and strong culture gives employees purpose, value and guidance for making key decisions. Continually investing in these areas is key; they will help guide the business through seasons of change. "
Dusty Wunderlich, Bristlecone Holdings

Little Wins
"It's easy to get sucked into the mentality of looking forward to the next big obstacle, especially when you're leading a startup. But it's very important for the morale of your company to stop and celebrate the little wins. Creating some sort of tradition — whether it's champagne or ringing a gong — will help give your team perspective and prevent burnout in the long run."
Mattan Griffel, One Month

Team Performance Evaluations
"When you're making money, everyone's work seems to be good and getting the job done. But sometimes what seems like 'getting the job done' is actually a market run that overlooks mistakes. Those same mistakes can come back to haunt you when that market slows unless you have consistently worked with your team to ensure that they are always operating at their best. This can be done through regular performance evaluations."
Rahim Charania, American Fueling Systems

Source: Adapted from The Young Entrepreneur Council (Dec 24, 2018) https://smallbiztrends.com/2015/04/growing-your-company.html, consulted in 23/8/2019.

As we can see, the main reasons for success depend strongly on context, timing and perspectives. For this reason, there is no magic formula that guarantees success. Rather, success comes down to a combination of several elements that align during a certain period and that allow the firm to leverage its skills.

What are the actions with higher impact for business growth?

There is a general agreement amongst business developers that there are four actions, which have a major impact on the promotion of business growth.

1. Attracting and keeping the right people. The core of each business is its people.
2. Establishing a truly differentiated strategy. Doing something differentiated from the competition, that really matters to customers.
3. Developing precise execution. Successfully performing a strategy requires complying with these three habits: set a handful of priorities, gather quantitative and qualitative data daily, and review weekly to guide decisions.
4. Navigating the financing process in advance. Planning financing for the long term, and not simply when the need arises.

What is the role of the comfort zone in business growth?

There is a global agreement that it not possible to grow a business without leaving one's comfort zone. However, our understanding is that growth forces a departure from the comfort zone. This means that all stakeholders need, at a certain point, to leave their own comfort zones, which subsequently encourages new ideas, the recognition of new opportunities, and, ultimately, innovation.

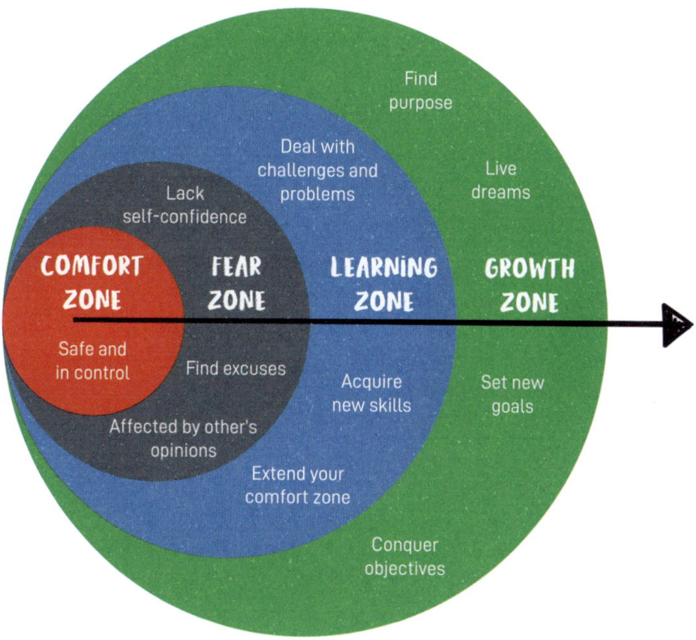

KEY IDEAS AND REFERENCES FOR MORE INFORMATION

- Several best practices proposed by entrepreneurs can be a good source of inspiration and for possible criteria for action
- People, Strategy, Execution and Money are the four keywords related to growth
- The management of the comfort zone is a very important leadership driver
- Innovation area is out of the comfort zone and "Innovation Happens When Ideas Have Sex" (Matt Ridley)

[1] Tilson, B. R. (2018) Go Slow To Grow Fast: How to Keep Your Company Driving And Thriving In A Fast-Paced, Competitive Business World, Forbes Books.

[2] McAlpine, G. (2017) Scale Up Millionaire: How To Sell Your Way To A Fast Growth, High Value Enterprise, Rethink Press Limited.

[3] Covey, S.R. (2013) The 7 Habits of Highly Effective People: Powerful Lessons in Personal Change, Simon & Schuster.

[4] Molinsky, A. (2017) Reach: A New Strategy to Help You Step Outside Your Comfort Zone, Rise to the Challenge and Build Confidence, Avery.

[5] Williams, P. (2018) Cadence: A Tale of Fast Business Growth. Morgan James Publishing.

[6] Anthony, S. (2017) The Little Black Book of Innovation, With a New Preface: How It Works, How to Do It, Harvard Business Review Press.

[7] Matt Ridley (2011) The Rational Optimist, Harper Perennial.

9

Why do some companies live longer?

What is the average lifespan of a company?

In 1958, the lifespan of a listed company was roughly 61 years. Today, in 2019, the average is just 18 years. At this rate, 75 per cent of the S&P 500 will be replaced by 2027. The reasons behind this shift are many, but in recent years, the advent of the Internet and cloud has reshaped how, when and where we do business. We currently live in an age where there is a noticeable wave of entrepreneurship, where there is a high growth rate and a high death rate. Eventually there will be a 'tipping point', and life expectancy for businesses will be higher in the mid to long term future.

Why do companies die?

Some authors believe it is possible to apply Darwinian evolution theory to business development and, thus firms need to do the same as successful species - keep their eyes and ears wide open for predators, and continually evolve what they do, through a process of constant adaptation and occasionally accelerated mutation. The chief factors among firms that endure include innovative capability, organisational systems, resources, organisational culture and strategy. These factors have also have a proven association with resilience, and a management style considered vogue-free and stable. The factors appear to be reliable ones, but the balance among them can change, depending on a set of conditions in the environment that managers should know how to scrutinise. Eventually, companies will die, and that is part of the course of life, both in species and in companies. The critical issue here is understanding this course of development, so that measures can be taken to cope with each change. Adaptation is, therefore, crucial.

Why is it important to understand the evolution of business longevity?

The S&P 500 or Standard & Poor's 500 Index is a market-capitalisation-weighted index of the 500 largest U.S. publicly traded companies. The 33-year average 'life expectancy' of companies on the S&P 500 in 1965 narrowed to 20 years in 1990 and is forecast to shrink to 14 years by 2026. The record of Mergers & Acquisitions activity and the growth of startups with multi-billion dollar valuations are leading indicators that a period of relative stability is ending, and that an increasing number of corporate leaders will lose control of their businesses' future.

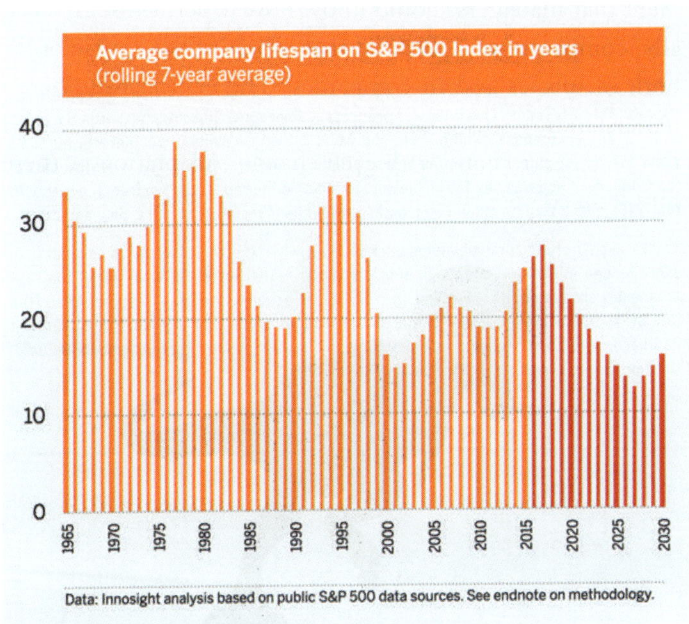

Which is the oldest European company?

The oldest European company - and the world's oldest limited liability corporation - is Stora Enso, a Swedish-Finnish renewable materials company, which started out in Sweden in 1288 as a mining company, before becoming a large paper and pulp manufacturer.

storaenso

THE RENEWABLE MATERIALS COMPANY

Stora Enso was formed in 1998 through the merger of the Finnish company Enso Oyj and the Swedish company Stora Kopparbergs Bergslags Aktiebolag (STORA).

With roots going back as far as the 1300's, Stora Enso has had many forms and diverse operations, overseas expansion, mergers and acquisitions, all the while meeting new business challenges. Change is very much a part of their heritage, and their ability to adapt has been the foundation of their endurance.

1288 is actually the first recorded documentation of Stora operations, namely copper mining near Falun, Sweden. This business progressed to become Stora Kopparbergs Bergslag in 1862, and encompass mining, iron, and wood activities. While it was several hundred years before any pulp, board or paper was produced, forestry was always a central part of the company. Wood was needed as fuel and for heating the copper or to extract the metal. In the 1970s, Stora sold its mining and metal operations to focus on forestry, pulp and paper.

The Enso part of the company dates back to 1872, when the W. Gutzeit & Co sawmill firm was founded in Kotka, Finland, by the Norwegian Hans Gutzeit. It was one of the first steam-powered sawmills in Finland. In 1912, Gutzeit acquired the Enso träsliperi AB. By the late 1990s, following a number of mergers and acquisitions over the years, Enso-Gutzeit had become Finland's largest forestry company. In 1996, after a merger with Veitsiluoto, the company took the name Enso Oy.

Today, the transformation continues, as Stora Enso focuses on all the possibilities of renewable materials, with the forest and trees as the foundation.

Source: adapted from www.storaenso.com, consulted in 15/6/2019.

What is the secret of business longevity?

As we have suggested, there is no single factor that impacts 'business longevity'. However the Darwinian concept of adaptation to the environment for a species in a specific niche can be applied to companies in specific business sectors and geographies. McKinsey conducted a deep analysis on this topic, from interviews with key executives. The following conditions relating to common business longevity factors were gathered:

- They are **relentless** and focus on their customers, and not just on their performance with customers but also on understanding what their best and most innovative customers are doing.
- They engage their **key suppliers** to solve problems and identify opportunities, so that these activities also become key sources of insight.
- They avoid introversion and actively seek to understand **broader trends** outside their own organisations and industries.
- They **challenge** legacy thinking and **legacy mind-sets**, encouraging and tolerating the cost of internal competition and cannibalisation.
- They avoid hubris, by creating a culture of dissatisfaction with current performance, however good.
- They adopt a predominantly "grow your own" talent philosophy to create a robust and loyal culture but mix it selectively and judiciously with external hires. In times of fundamental and disruptive change, enduring companies must be willing to change their management.

- They **do not tolerate** extended tenures in top-management roles.
- They focus relentlessly on values and constantly demonstrate why their corporate values matter - and why, to be meaningful, must be reflected in the key managerial processes, such as performance evaluation and appointments
- They encourage their boards to play an active but supportive role in challenging priorities and the status quo, particularly in times of success.

What are the characteristics of companies that lived more than 100 years?

A study of over 100 companies with lifespans of more than 100 years - from a universe of 206 companies in 2014 in Portugal (info from D&B Informa database - www.informadb.pt) - showed that old companies did not have one sole characteristic that promoted longevity. Old companies should be considered 'protected species', taking into account their singularities: they display characteristics, which deserve to be further studied in the pursuit of better understanding and benchmarking.

The analysis of history, shareholders, financials and sector framework interaction showed that to a larger or smaller extent these firms had five common characteristics:

1. They were **specialised** with a specific portfolio (they operated mainly in just a single sector or, sometimes, in a specific area of the value chain)

2. They always had a focus on quality/**excellence** (normally, they were the first, or the best at doing something)
3. The main criteria for management related to **trust** lines (they are, or were for a long time, family businesses, and preserved as that)
4. They had a business DNA which was very strong in **tradition and business culture** (all of them showed the capacity to learn from history and market outcomes)
5. They had moments where they **re-invented** themselves in order **to adapt** to the challenges of their frameworks (they constantly adapted to new realities)

These conclusions cannot be applied widely to all contexts and markets, or even to different countries, but they show a pattern that can be found in other western countries where many 'old' companies exist.

KEY IDEAS AND REFERENCES FOR MORE INFORMATION

- The capacity to re-invent in order to adapt to new circumstances is one of the most important drivers for longevity. This requires recognition of the need for re-invention
- Business culture and their business DNA is of critical importance for the establishment of an organisation's model and set of values.
- Old companies are focused and always want to be the first, the best or the biggest at something that is relevant for a segment of the market

[1] Davis, I. (2014). Reflections on corporate longevity. McKinsey Quarterly, 3(3), 118-122.
[2] Anthony, S. D., Viguerie, S. P., and Waldeck, A. (2016). Corporate longevity: Turbulence ahead for large organizations. Strategy & Innovation, 14 (1), 1-9.
[3] Galadanchi, H. A. and Julienti, A. B. (2018), A Study of Factors That Support Longevity of Business Enterprises, OSR Journal of Business and Management, Vol. 20 (1), pp. 53-59.

10

What are gazelle companies? And what can we learn from them?

What is a gazelle company?

A gazelle company or simply, gazelle, is a young, very fast-growing company. A company is considered a gazelle if it has an annual growth rate of 20% or more, as measured by sales revenue. Typically, these are small publicly-traded companies that have sustained this level of growth for each of the past four years, beginning with sales of at least $1 million. In addition, gazelle companies are often known for creating many new job opportunities.

Gazelle Companies

According to the original technical definition, a gazelle company is a high-growth company that has been increasing its revenues by at least 20% annually for four years or more, starting from a revenue base of at least $100,000. This pace of growth means that the company has effectively more than doubled its revenues over a four-year period. As gazelle companies are characterised by their rapid pace of sales growth, rather than their absolute size, they can range in size from small companies to very large enterprises, though a majority of them are on the smaller end of the scale.

The author and economist David Birch first coined the term "gazelle" in some of his early studies on employment and introduced his concept to a wider audience in his 1987 book, "Job Creation in America: How Our Smallest Companies Put the Most People to Work."

Source: adapted from www.investopedia.com/terms/g/gazellecompany.asp, consulted in 23/8/2019.

Why are gazelle companies relevant to 'segment' growth?

Gazelle companies are often used to characterise corporate growth in different regions. The concept is very well fitted to segment growth. It is useful to investigate the key components of great businesses that succeed in taking their company from millions to billions - and equally, ask why some companies fail to make it despite having appeared to possess all the ingredients for success.

Gazelle companies in the Life Cycle of Companies

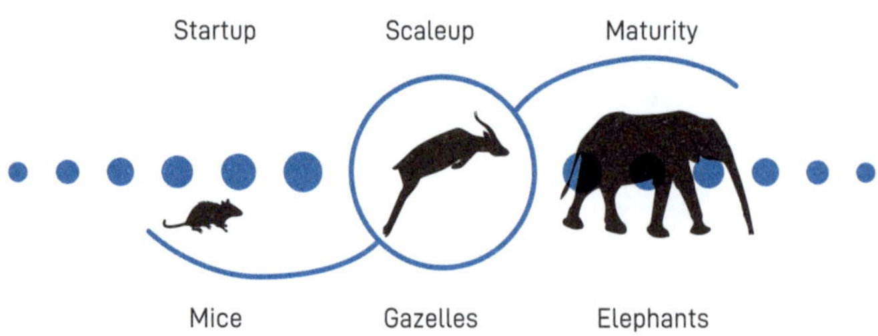

Source: adapted from [4].

What are the key characteristics of gazelle companies?

There are common features of gazelles that might explain their success. Several studies show that in most gazelle companies, employees are their economic engines. Half of them appear to consider entrepreneurship as a passion, and some make reference to their employees' commitment. They all seem to have created a unique and well-defined business concept. Their business mission corresponds with their daily activity and is constantly modified.

Rapid-growing companies also have a common focus on their core activities, and offer their clients overall solutions. These companies also tend to be innovators in their industries and are always a step ahead of their rivals. Moreover, they are all conscious of their core competencies and aware of which core processes creates the most value for customers and are most competitively unique. They tend to have a divisional form of organisation and straight communication within the company. Creating a good reputation seems to be more important than marketing, in itself.

They also have the following features in common, as driving forces in their business activities: entrepreneurship, creativity, innovating power and a lot of ambition. A common characteristic is that they often obtain a niche in the market and create new opportunities and sales avenues, and additionally, they achieve wealth potential through long term contracts or/and partnerships with customers and suppliers.

Why are gazelle companies such a relevant research topic?

Gazelle companies are relevant because they generate much more employment than other companies and deliver high returns to their shareholders. The main factors that explain their success are competitive advantages based on human resources, innovation, internationalisation, excellence in their processes and a conservative financial policy.

Gazelle companies show the dynamics of a region or sector. The existence (quantity) and level (performance) of gazelle companies in a certain region or sector demonstrates vitality and growth potential. The emulation of gazelle companies is often a good benchmarking option. Gazelle companies can be a very good tool for teaching and learning.

KEY IDEAS AND REFERENCES FOR MORE INFORMATION

- Attracting and keeping the right People
- Creating a truly differentiated Strategy
- Driving flawless Execution
- Having plenty of Cash to weather the storms

[1] Birch, D. L. (1987) Job Creation in America: How Our Smallest Companies Put the Most People to Work, Free Press.

[2] Borgström, H. and Kloutschek, E. (2005). The successful elements of the Gazelles-A case-study of Gary Hamel's Business Model applied to rapid-growing companies in the region of Gothenburg.

[3] Harnish, V. (2014). Scaling up. Gazelles Inc, Ashburn, VA.

[4] Collins, J. (2016). Good to Great: Why Some Companies Make the Leap and Others Don't. Instaread.

[5] Hamel, G. & Breen, B. (2007). Building an innovation democracy: WL Gore. The future of management, Harvard Business School Press.

11

What are unicorn companies? And what can we learn from them?

What is a unicorn company?

The term 'unicorn' has different meanings in the business world. In the venture capital industry, a unicorn refers to any tech startup company that reaches a $1billion market value as determined by private or public investment. The term was coined in 2013 by Aileen Lee, founder of Cowboy Ventures, who chose the mythical animal to represent the statistical rarity of such successful ventures.

A 'decacorn' is a word used for those companies valued at over $10 billion, while 'hectocorn' is the appropriate term for such a company valued over $100 billion. According to VentureBeat, there were 229 unicorns as of January 2016. The largest unicorns included Uber, Xiaomi, Airbnb, Palantir, Snapchat, Dropbox and Pinterest.

Aileen Lee (1970-present) serves as the Founder and Partner at Cowboy Ventures. She founded it in 2012 and also served as its Managing Director. She is lead or supporting partner in backing a broad variety of companies like Bloom Energy. Currently, she serves as a Director of Texito, Inc., and others. She serves as the Director at Bricksolve, Inc. and Tally Technologies, Inc. Aileen Lee Lee has been a Director of Hua Yuan Science and Technology Association since January 2006.

Lee has appeared on Forbes' list of The World's 100 Most Powerful Women (position #93) and its The Top Women Investors On Midas In 2018 list (position #97), and on the Times list of 100 Most Influential People in 2019.

Why are unicorns important?

Why do investors seem to care about "billion dollar exits"? Historically, top venture funds have driven returns from their ownership in just a few companies in a given fund of many companies. Plus, traditional venture funds have grown in size, requiring larger "exits" to deliver acceptable returns.

To answer these questions, the Cowboy Ventures team built a dataset of U.S.-based tech companies started since January 2003 and most recently valued at $1 billion by private or public markets. This was called the "Learning Project", and is ongoing, which means data is constantly being gathered and can be accessed.

What can growing businesses learn from unicorns?

A growing business can view unicorns as inspiring organisations. There are many specific characteristics that can be of relevance:

- Every major technology wave has given birth to one or more super-unicorns
- Consumer-oriented companies have created the majority of value in the past decade
- Enterprise-oriented unicorns have delivered more value per private dollar invested
- Four primary business models drive value, and network effects help
- It's a marathon, not a sprint: it takes 7+ years to get to a "liquidity event"
- The twenty-something inexperienced founder is an outlier, not the norm
- The "big pivot" is also an outlier, especially for enterprise companies
- The Bay Area, especially San Francisco, is home to the vast majority of unicorns
- There is A LOT of opportunity to bring diversity into the founders club
- Not their first rodeo: founders have lots of startup and tech experience
- Nearly 80 percent of unicorns had at least one co-founder who had previously founded a company of some sort.
- Some founders showed their entrepreneurial DNA as early as junior high.

- The list of prior startups co-founded spans failure and success.
- The majority of founding CEOs, and 90 percent of enterprise CEOs have technical degrees from college.

Learnings to date about the "Unicorn Club"

The evaluation of 39 companies belonging to what is called "the Unicorn Club" were evaluated (by definition, U.S.-based software companies started since 2003 and valued at over $1 billion by public or private market investors). That is about 0.07% of venture-backed consumer and enterprise software startups.

On average, four unicorns were born per year in the past decade, with Facebook being the breakout "super-unicorn" (worth >$100 billion). In each recent decade, 1-3 super unicorns have been born.

Consumer-oriented unicorns have been more plentiful and created more value in aggregate, even excluding Facebook. But enterprise-oriented unicorns have become worth more on average, and raised much less private capital, delivering a higher return on private investment.

Unicorn Companies fall somewhat evenly into four major business models:

1. Consumer e-commerce,
2. Consumer audience,
3. Software-as-a-service
4. Enterprise software.

Companies with well-educated, thirty-something co-founders who have history together have built the most successes. The "big pivot" after starting with a different initial product is an outlier.

San Francisco (not the Valley) now reigns as the home of unicorns. Thus, to create fields where Unicorn companies can evolve is very important for policy makers in the field of business development.

There is very little diversity among founders in the Unicorn Club.

Source: adapted from: https://techcrunch.com/2013/11/02/welcome-to-the-unicorn-club/, consulted in 24/8/2019.

KEY IDEAS AND REFERENCES FOR MORE INFORMATION

- The unicorns have many smaller business as suppliers and often they buy other companies complimentary to their business
- The understanding of unicorn phenomena is very important for policy makers in the fields of economic development
- Eventually it is possible to create an environment that enables the emergence of unicorns

[1] Manjoo, F. (5 July 2015). "Unicorn: A Fitting Label for Its Time and Place". NY Times. The New York Times.

[2] Chaykowski, K. (3 April 2018), "Meet The Top Women Investors On Midas In 2018", Forbes.

[3] Mitra, S. (2014) Billion Dollar Unicorns: Entrepreneur Journeys Kindle Edition.

[4] Bhatia, R. (2019) Startup Idea To IPO: What does it take to create a Unicorn Company, Adhyyan Books.

[5] Lee, A. (2013) Welcome To The Unicorn Club: Learning From Billion-Dollar Startups, available at https://techcrunch.com/2013/11/02/welcome-to-the-unicorn-club/ consulted in 24/8/2019.

12

What are the common characteristics of inspiring and fast-growing companies?

What is business traction?

Traction is a very common keyword when it comes to business incubators and accelerators. When a business is pitching for funding, a common question that investors will ask concerns precisely the achievement of market traction. Market traction is just one factor that determines a venture capitalist or business angel's interest in funding a business; however, it can be a very important one. In fact, finding enough capital to fund a developing business and keep it running can be difficult for a company that has not had sufficient time to prove itself in the marketplace. By creating business traction, new companies can attract potential investors and gain a competitive edge in their industry.

Traction is often regarded as the first of three phases of growing of a startup. This is followed by Transition and

Growth. During each of these phases, everything (for example, metrics, channels, focus, and team structure) evolves and changes. Knowing where our business is on this path helps to understand where we should be focusing our attention, and choose the right tactics at the right time. This is why it is important to understand the differences between each phase and understand that this can vary depending on the type of business.

	Traction	Transition	Growth
Goal	Product — Market fit	Discovering Growth levers	Turning up Growth levers
Metric	Retention	Growth Rate	Growth Rate
Volume	Turn on faucet Find steady minimum stream	Turn up faucet	Firehorse
Channels	Experiment with 2-3 in order to find focus on 1	1	1+
Optimization	Macro	Macro + Micro	Micro
Team	•	• •••	• ••• ••• ••• •••

Source: adapted from https://brianbalfour.com/essays/traction-vs-growth, consulted in 24/8/2019.

What does fast-growing mean? How does it compare with hypergrowth?

The term "hypergrowth" is recent and the first significant mention of it comes from an April 2008 issue of the Harvard Business Review, which defined it as being "the steep part of the S-curve that most young markets and industries experience at some point, where the winners get sorted from the losers". For example, in contrast to normal growth firms, scalability is the key priority for Hypergrowth companies, and our findings indicate that agility is often a naturally embedded cultural priority for Hypergrowth companies, and thus receives less direct attention than one might anticipate.

Achieving hypergrowth means maintaining a 40%+ average annual growth rate for more than one year. On another hand, "rapid growth" companies are defined as having a CAGR of between 20% and 40%, while "normal growth" companies have CAGRs of less than 20%. "Hypergrowth" became jargon for very fast growth and was adopted by the business development community. It is said that hypergrowth either kills a company or makes it much stronger.

What is CAGR?

CAGR is the acronym Compound Annual Growth Rate and it defines the rate of return that would be required for an investment to grow from its starting balance to its end balance, assuming the profits were reinvested at the end of each year of the investment's lifespan. Hence, it is a business-and-investing-specific term for the geometric progression ratio that provides a constant rate of return over a period of time. CAGR is considered to be the best formula for evaluating how different investments have performed over time.

To determine CAGR, one needs a start value, and end value, and the amount of time between these values. It can be calculated as follows: divide the value of an investment at the end of the period in question by its value at the beginning of that period, raise the result to the power of one divided by the period length, and subtract one from the subsequent result.

$$\text{CAGR Formula} = \left[\left(\frac{\text{Ending Value}}{\text{Beginning Value}}\right)^{\frac{1}{\text{No. of Years}}} - 1\right] \times 100\%$$

What are the most relevant factors for business growth?

There are no magical drivers that, once applied, will promote business growth. However, there are normally two factors common to all examples of fast business growth leaders: leadership (see Vol. 1 – BCR) is one of them. However, this needs to be backed up by a good management team. In addition to this, momentum needs to be considered (see Vol. 2 – BCR). This latter aspect refers to the ability to understand the alignment of forces that push for action in the right moment and at the right time. We will develop the aspect related to management.

What does the expression "Level 5 leadership" mean?

Level 5 leadership is a concept developed in the book *Good to Great* (Collins, 2001). Level 5 leaders display a powerful mixture of personal humbleness and indomitable will. They are incredibly ambitious, but their ambition is first and foremost for the cause, for the organisation and its purpose, not for themselves. While Level 5 leaders can come in many personality packages, they are often self-effacing, quiet, reserved, and even shy. Every good-to-great transition seems to have begun with a Level 5 leader, who motivated the entire company more with inspired standards than with what could be described as an inspiring personality.

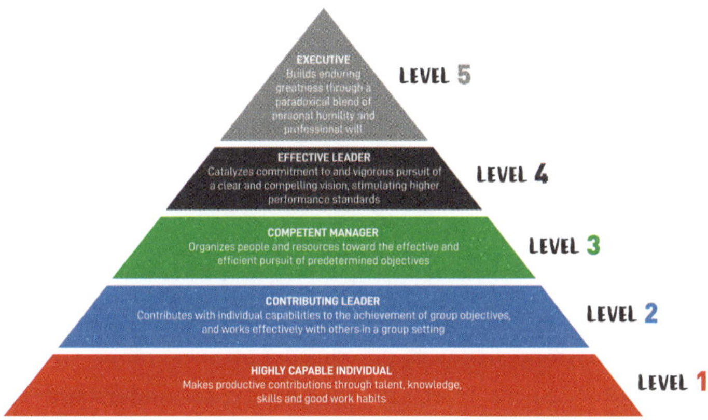

This type of leadership normally develops within a unique and inspiring work context, characterised by business intent, customer connection, and employee experience. These are not simply cultural norms designed to shape behaviour. In this context, employees connect with a galvanising idea, with the notion of service to end users, and with the distinctive, intrinsic rewards of life on the job. This way, people form emotional ties to the company, and those ties energise the organization.

What is the role of management in growth?

As we have already suggested, growth processes start normally with a substantial dose of good leadership. Besides that, management is fundamental. Managers are the people who make things happen in the firm and there seems to be consensus that their role is capital. However, this hasn't always been the case, Google attempted to check it in a project that started in 2002.

Google initiated a project in 2002 to try to understand the role of managers: the **Google Oxygen project**. Back then, they attempted to prove that managers did not really matter in the development of a business. After obtaining the results, Google re-considered their theory that managers could be reduced to a minimum. Instead, they discovered eight traits of the very best ones. These were considered essential to make a great manager. The hypothesis was that the quality of a manager did not matter, and that managers were at best a necessary evil, and at worst, a useless layer of bureaucracy.

The whole idea behind the Oxygen Project was a radical experiment — a move to a flat organisation without any managers, but mainly engineers. Google's experiment lasted only a few months, as Google found employees were left without direction and guidance for their most basic questions and needs. The whole experiment was considered a failure. However, on the basis of this experience, Google pivoted to extensively study the opposite question: what were the common behaviours of their very best managers? With this first experiment, it was possible to identify the eight behaviours common among the highest performing managers, and incorporate them into manager development programs. Publicising and training managers in these eight behaviours aimed an improvement in management at Google aimed, namely, in terms of team outcomes such as turnover, satisfaction, and performance over time. Later, two additional characteristics emerged as being relevant. It was then that the company was able to list the 10 characteristics it believed made for the best managers:

Managements skills for Managers based on Google research
1. Be a good coach. A leader can choose whether to care about the employees or not. If the decision is to care, then time and energy should be invested in helping employees to become better versions of themselves. This is part of being a good coach. Another condition for being a good coach involves the understanding of the leader role as being a facilitator, and not a fixer. Thus, asking good questions, defining challenges and not simply giving answers or solving problems, is fundamental.
2. Empower teams and do not micromanage. Empowered employees have higher job satisfaction and commitment to the organisation, which reduces turnover and increases performance and motivation. In addition, supervisors who empower are regarded as more influential and inspiring by their subordinates, rather than leaders who micromanage and limit freedom.

3. Create an inclusive team environment, showing concern for success and well-being. Displaying concern for the success of the team is important and individual fulfilment is often a joint effort between all members of a team. People derive tremendous joy from being part of a winning team. The best managers facilitate esprit de corps and interdependence. Moreover, employees respond to managers who are concerned about winning and winning well (in a way that supports their well-being).
4. Be productive and results oriented. Productivity of employees should be considered in a serious way, which means that tools should be provided so as to guarantee achievement and avoid overloading and tasks overlapping.
5. Be a good communicator - listen and share information. The biggest problem with communication is the illusion that it has taken place, when it reality, it has not. Often it does not happen because of a lack of effort from both sides: both the sender and receiver of the message. Therefore, investing in communication is important, as well as devoting time to listen. Also important is the anticipation of all topics that need to be communicated instead of focusing attention solely on the first one, not allowing the receiver to understand that there are other messages to pass on.
6. Have a clear vision/strategy for the team. If we don't know where we want to go, any road will take us there. Therefore, guidance is crucial in management. A guarantee that the right guidance is being passed on is also fundamental. For this to happen, employees should be enrolled in building a vision/strategy; simply imposing things on them should be avoided. This way, the leader is creating both commitment and compliance.
7. Support career development and discuss performance. The best managers care about their people's careers and development as much as they care about their own. People crave feedback, and that should be owed to them. People work to bring meaning into their lives, and meaning comes from personal growth and development; career perspective is therefore fundamental.
8. Have the expertise to advise the team. The firm should want its managers to have key technical skills, so they can share the "been there, done that" experience. For that to happen, education and training, as well as experience are crucial. This way, employees expect to build up their own core expertise, whatever that might be. To promote this, leaders should also be in tune with the latest trends in technology and innovation.
9. Collaborate. In a global and remote business world, collaboration skills are essential. Collaboration happens when each team member feels accountability and interdependence with teammates. Nothing is more destructive for a team than a leader who is unwilling to collaborate. It creates a "it's up to only us" vibe that kills culture, productivity, and results.
10. Be a strong decision maker. The alternative is indecision, which paralyses an organisation, creates doubt, uncertainty, lack of focus, and even resentment. Strong decisions come from a strong sense of self-confidence and belief that a decision, even if proved wrong, is better than none.

Source: adapted from adapted from: https://rework.withgoogle.com/blog/the-evolution-of-project-oxygen/, assessed at 20/7/2019.

KEY IDEAS AND REFERENCES FOR MORE INFORMATION

- The inspiring businesses are unique
- Culture-based leadership is in the DNA of inspiring businesses and that is what makes them inspiring and distinct
- Growth is strongly dependent on a leadership supported by management

[1] Collins, J. (2011) Good to Great, Harper Business.

[2] Izosimov, A. V. (2008). Managing hypergrowth. Harvard Business Review, 86(4), 121

[3] Northouse, P. G. (2017). Introduction to leadership: Concepts and practice. Sage Publications.

[4] Rumelt, R. P. (2012). Good strategy/bad strategy: The difference and why it matters. Strategic Direction, 28(8).

[5] Jocko Willink and Leif Babin (2018) The Dichotomy of Leadership: Balancing the Challenges of Extreme Ownership to Lead and Win, Mcmillan US.

[6] John C. Maxwell (2013)The 5 Levels of Leadership: Proven Steps to Maximize Your Potential, Center Street; Reprint edition.

13

What are the most common business failure factors?

What is a business failure?

A business failure is a situation in which a company or any type of business ceases operations because it is unable to generate sufficient revenue to cover its expenses. Business failure is relatively common in the first year or so of operations because the business leaders are unable to drive the organisation to compete for several reasons. Very often, a business failure or death can be regarded as just a step in the business's life cycle.

> Business failure is a frequent situation that results from fast growth. Therefore, it is very important to understand all the factors that can contribute to business failure, in order to avoid them and manage when they arrive.

What are the most relevant business failure factors?

Evaluation of the main sources referring to reasons for business failure shows that the most frequently-cited reasons relate to communication. This is does not necessarily mean that there was a marketing problem but that there might have been a wrong momentum-related decision. When businesses do not follow a path with an appropriate roadmap based on validation steps, they tend to fail.

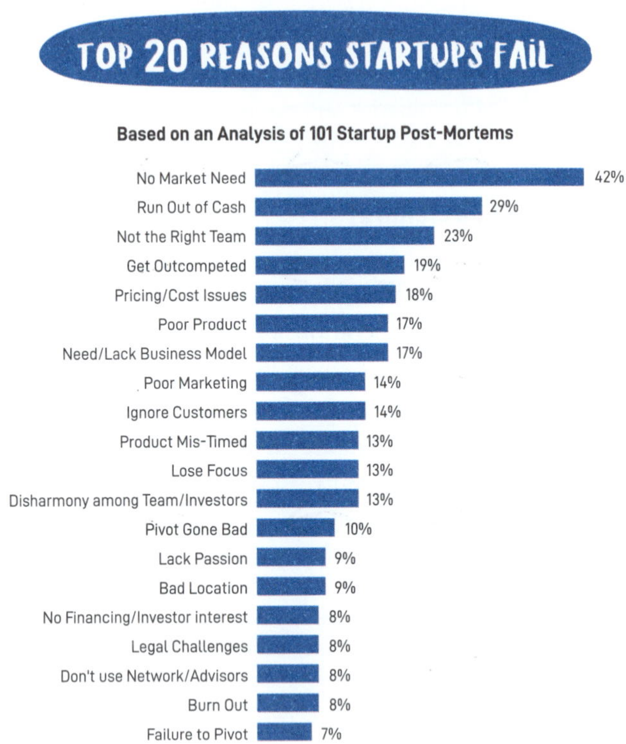

Source: adapted from www.cbinsights.com/research/startup-failure-reasons-top/, accessed at 20/7/2019.

The business = Leaders + Followers	• Flow of accurate information • Appropriate understanding about information • Management use of the information	The Market = Clients + Competitors

What are the common management mistakes in startups?

Understanding common mistakes, as identified by business analysts and consultants, can provide a good basis for entrepreneurs' decisions. The most common mistake is the underestimation of the relevance of the team from the start. The different 'mistakes' have a different relevance depending on the nature of the business, the business framework and the momentum.

1. Single Founder
2. Bad location
3. Marginal Niche
4. Derivative Idea
5. Obstinacy
6. Hiring bad Programmers
7. Choosing the Wrong Platform
8. Slowness in Launching
9. Launching too early
10. Having No specific user in mind
11. Raising too little money
12. Spending too much
13. Raising too much money
14. Poor Investor management
15. Sacrificing User to (supposed) Profit
16. Not wanting to get your hands dirty
17. Fighting between Founders
18. A half-hearted effort

Source: adapted from www.inc.com/larry-kim/avoid-these-18-entrepreneurial-mistakes-for-a-more-successful-start-up.html, accessed in 20/7/2019.

How can business failure be avoided?

There are no magic formulae to avoid mistakes, except doing nothing in the first place. However, it is good practice to know which are the most common business failures, and incorporate that information in the genesis of the business, so the organisation is designed to overcome these problems from the beginning.

7 Failures of Business Growth by Daniel Burrus (FEBRUARY 6, 2019)
FAILURE TO ANTICIPATE Most companies react to change as it occurs. You must anticipate and plan for future changes. You can anticipate a great deal in your industry. For example, are automobiles of the future mostly going to be electric instead of gas? Many think so. Could automobiles hover like drones instead of drive on four wheels? Of course! Instead of being a crisis manager and reacting to change, anticipate changes so you can drive growth from the inside out. Spend one hour a week focusing on predictable opportunities to strategise and become more of an opportunity management organisation.
FAILURE TO COMMUNICATE There is a difference between informing and communicating. Informing is one-way and static, and seldom leads to action. Communicating is two-way and dynamic, and usually leads to action. We have these fantastic Communication Age tools but use them in an Information Age way. If you cannot communicate internally with your staff, how can you communicate externally with customers and shareholders? When you focus on maximising two-way communication, you can create a Communication Age organisation and accelerate positive change.
FAILURE TO COLLABORATE The majority of people tend to cooperate, which is a lower-level function, different from collaboration. Even though we often use the word "collaborate," we frequently really just mean, "cooperate". Cooperation means, "I won't get in your way if you won't get in mine." Such an approach produces results but certainly not outstanding results, because it's based on a scarcity mentality. Collaboration is instead based on abundance and gets competitors to work with you rather than against you. It occurs when we put our heads together and ask ourselves, "How can we create a bigger pie for everyone?"

FAILURE TO INNOVATE

When asked what their last big innovation was, most companies have to go back five or ten years to cite something meaningful, as the majority of companies innovate once, form a company around the innovation, and then let it ride. They stop innovating and instead spend a great deal of effort asking themselves how they can become more efficient by doing more with less, reducing overhead, and using technology better. You must ask yourself how you can use technology and staff to create new products and services to increase sales all around. Innovation fuels profitability and efficiency.

FAILURE TO PRE-SOLVE PROBLEMS

Always remember that a problem is not an opportunity in disguise; it is a problem! A problem is only an opportunity before it occurs, and most problems we experience are predictable. If you ask customers what they want and then give it to them, you are missing the real opportunity. Instead, you need to think at a level higher and ask yourself and your customers, "What problems are we about to have?" Develop new solutions based on those answers and base your product development on your customer's future problems.

FAILURE TO DE-COMMODITISE

Unfortunately, most companies come up with something new and make it their main product. Other companies copy the product, and then market saturation occurs. Try de-commoditising your offering by taking your product and putting a service wrapper around it. For example, in the electricity industry, the utility provider cannot increase prices without permission from ratepayers. One electric company bypassed this limitation by creating what it calls "digital electricity." They sold customers a product that, for a higher cost, prevented any fluctuation of voltage from occurring. Many big companies signed up for this more expensive service, and in the near future, homeowners with streaming devices will have a similar interest. This electric utility took a product and wrapped a service around it in order to de-commoditise.

FAILURE TO DIFFERENTIATE

Too many companies become just like everyone else. True strategic planning needs to be more than numbers-based; it needs to focus on how you can differentiate your company and products from those of the competition. You differentiate by avoiding all the failure modes we have discussed that prevent business growth. You anticipate, communicate, collaborate, innovate, pre-problem solve, and de-commoditise. Become what your competition is not, in order to differentiate.

Source: adapted from. https://www.burrus.com/2019/02/7-failures-of-business-growth/, consulted in 20/7/2019.

Daniel Burrus (born in 1947) is an American technology futurist, innovation expert, business adviser, author, and public speaker in the areas of business strategy and innovation. He attended The Wisconsin State University-Oshkosh, where he graduated in 1971 with a bachelor's degree. He has written on the topics of business transformation and technology-driven trends.

He is the creator of the Hard Trend Methodology and the Anticipatory Organization® Business Model now being used by leading organisations worldwide. His accurate predictions date back to the early 1980s when he became the first and only futurist to accurately identify the 20 exponential technologies that would become the driving force of business and economic growth for decades to come.

What should we do when business failure happens?

The failure rate of startups is relatively high, especially for first-time entrepreneurs. Roughly, 50% of all small businesses fail within the first four years, and many of those are started by first-timers, who have limited entrepreneurial, business, or management experience. Even when there is a fantastic idea, a dedicated team to make that idea a reality, and a plan for most contingencies, external factors that cannot be controlled, and a lack of overall experience can cause the business to collapse. Even if this is not the case, other aspects related to infrastructure, leadership and communication might hinder the continuation of the business.

In reality, failure is a real possibility for the vast majority of business owners.

What should we do if and when failure happens?
1. Analyse the failure. Avoid taking business failure personally.
3. Work with other entrepreneurs. Learn from failure.
4. Take time out. Take things one-step at a time.
6. Look for proper advice to avoid becoming stuck on a course of negative thinking.
5. Start thinking about a new business plan.
2. Get our finances in order. Prepare for a new venture or the next stage in our life.

These five steps can help to accept the failure and move on. It is very important to reflect on what went wrong and find solutions to the problem that caused the failure. It is also crucial to learn from the mistakes and do things differently the next time. Another important piece of advice is to draw inspiration from people who failed many times but eventually achieved their dreams, and learn from their experience. When moving on to bigger and better opportunities, we should make sure we also take advantage of the experience we've gained in the process. This is the keystone of experience and it starts with admitting what we did wrong.

KEY IDEAS AND REFERENCES FOR MORE INFORMATION

- Business failure is always a possibility and the only way to avoid it is doing nothing
- It is possible to learn from common failures and avoid or manage them when they happen
- There is an important body of knowledge about best practices related with business development to avoid common failure factors

[1] Clark, C. and Kelly, J. (2016) Start Here: The World's Best Business Growth & Consulting Book: Business Growth Strategies from The World's Best Business Coach

[2] Rose, D. S. and Gross, B. (2016) The Startup Checklist: 25 Steps to a Scalable, High-Growth Business, John Wiley & Sond, New Jersey.

[3] Anofienem, U. (2019) Best Business Growth Advice from World's Greatest Entrepreneurs, Kindle Ed.

[4] Michalowicz, M. (2018) Clockwork: Design Your Business to Run Itself, Portfolio.

[5] Burrus, D. (2017) Anticipatory Organization: : Turn Disruption and Change into Opportunity and Advantage, Greenleaf Book Group Press.

14

How can disruptive business models be adapted for any business?

What are business models? How can we adapt them?

A business model can be defined as a process to develop the successful operation of a business, identifying the sources of revenue, the intended customer base, products, and details of financing. A business model is basically the company's plan for making a profit. The most well-known definition of a 'business model' was proposed by Alexander Osterwalder: "*A business model describes the rationale of how an organisation creates, delivers, and captures value, in economic, social, cultural or other contexts.* The process of business model construction is part of business strategy". (in Osterwalder et al. (2010) Business Model Generation).

Business = Exchange. There are many ways to exchange a product or service for a benefit that, most of the time, is monetary. The **exchange process** is in the core of the business model and the important question is how to adapt it for different business. The adaptation might require simulation, trials and validation. (see The BCR, Vol. 1).

What are the different types of business models?

A business is an exchange and the model describes the process of exchange. Therefore we can group the businesses models into three groups according to the process of exchange: (1) levelled purchase; (2) Repeated purchase; and (3) Fractionated purchase. (More detail can be found in The BCR, Vol. 2.)

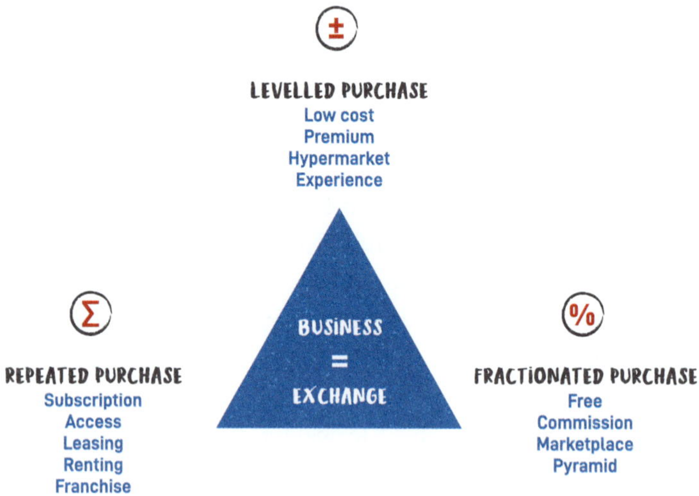

Is it possible to have more than one business model for the same business?

Yes. A global business model can be a blend of different specific business models put together.

This can be done at different moments in time, in different markets and in different locations. Knowing the business model is also of capital importance for investors, as with this information they may have an idea about how the growth of the business will happen. Successful businesses often combine several business models.

Business models need to be validated and a way of starting the process is with prototyping and/or simulation.

What are the common factors for all business models?

It is possible to say that all business models concern either a product, a service, or both. They may be B2B or B2C, or both, combined. They must refer to the nature of the transaction. The trade or exchange process is the core of the model and the exchange platform might be an ecosystem with few or many players. Each type of exchange happens in a specific framework and requires, as we have already said, a validation process before adoption.

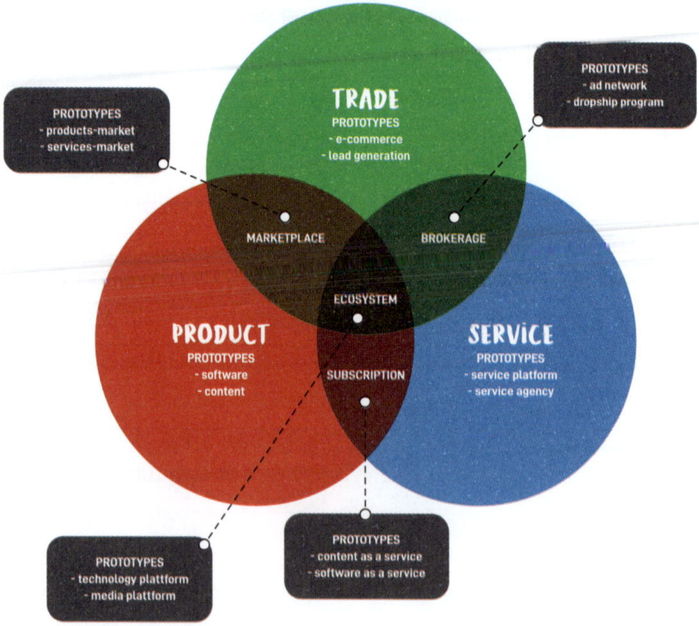

What are disruptive business models? How can we use them for growth?

Disruptive business models are exchange processes that can bring innovative or out-of-the-box approaches to a specific business. The model in itself - because it is based on an exchange - can be as old as humankind, but the disruption should be there: this can be in the way it is implemented and/or in the way, it is combined with other business models. The use of digital platforms is a disruptive way to implement old ways of doing business. The listing of the different disruptive business models is a possible way to understand how they can be adapted for different realities. (For this purpose, see The BCR, Vol. 2.)

10 Hyper disruptive business models with examples
1. **Subscription**. A regular product or service sale (subscription) that replaces an ad-hoc purchase Examples: NetFlix, Dollar, Apple Music
2. **Free.** Transform non-paying users into suppliers of something that others will pay for (remember: if you are not paying for the product you are the product) Examples: Google, Facebook, Instagram
3. **Freemium.** Free model plus subscription model (1+2) Examples: Spotify, Linkedin, Dropbox
4. **On-demand**. From people with time and no money to people with no time and with money Examples: Uber, Operator, Taskrabbit, Paypal
5. **Access.** Temporary access over ownership through monetisation of goods and services in a sharing economy Examples: Zipcar, Peerbuy, AirbnB
6. **Experience** . Provide a superior experience where payment results from exceeded expectations Examples: Tesla, Apple
7. **Pyramid.** Resellers and affiliates who get a commission International examples: Amazon, Microsoft, Dropbox,
8. **Marketplace.** A placement fee or commission in exchange for connecting buyers and sellers directly APPROPRIATE FOR LARGE COMPANIES Examples: eBay, iTunes, AirBnB, Farfetch
9. **Hypermarket.** Bombing with scale to sell with reduced prices APPROPRIATE FOR LARGE COMPANIES Examples: Amazon, Apple, Prozis
10. **Ecosystem.** Consumer dependency on an interlocked and interdependent suite of products and services APPROPRIATE FOR LARGE COMPANIES Examples: Apple, Google, Nike, Nestlé with Nespresso

Source: adapted from https://www.digitaltransformationbook.com, consulted in 29/9/2019.

What other business models can be adapted for most businesses?

There are several other business models that can provide inspiration when improving a business model. It is good practice to do our 'homework' and evaluate the most relevant business models used in a specific sector and related ones, and those that might emerge in the future.

Franchise business model This is the practice of using a successful business model — for the franchisor, the franchise is an alternative to building 'chain stores' to distribute goods and avoid investment and liability over a chain. The franchisor's success is the success of the franchisees. Examples: Subway, 7-Eleven, McDonalds
Bricks and clicks business model A company integrates both offline (bricks) and online (clicks) presences. This happens when a chain of stores allows the user to order products online, but lets them pick up their order at a local store. Examples: El corte Inglès (Click and go), Leroy Merlin, Inditex (Zara), Auchan (Jumbo), Zilian
Collective business models Typically composed of relatively large numbers of businesses, tradespeople or professionals in the same or related fields of endeavour, which pools resources, shares information or provides other benefits. Science parks or high-tech campus, for instance, provide shared resources (e.g. cleanrooms and other lab facilities) to the firms located on its premises, and, in addition, seeks to create an innovation community among these firms and their employees. Examples: Tek Office
Servitisation of products business model. Transforming costs of purchase in rentals with service — mostly related to financial services, hospitality, retail, health, information technology and education. Examples: IBM (it treats its products business as a service business. Although it still manufactures computers, it sees the physical goods as a small part of the "business solutions" industry), Google, and leasing and renting examples in the car industry.
The premium business model This business model seeks a higher profit margin on a lower sales volume. It is the concept of offering high end products and services appealing to discriminating consumers. Brand image is an important factor, as quality is often a subjective matter. Examples: Rolls-Royce, BMW and Mercedes-Benz in the auto industry, Gucci bags and Rolex watches in the luxury accessories industry, and elite personal services such as using a chauffeur, Fashion Clinique, The Yeatman Hotels.
Pay what you can (PWYC) business model This asks customers to pay what they feel the product or service is worth to them. It is often used as a promotional tactic, but can also be the regular method of doing business. It is a variation on the gift economy and cross-subsidisation, in that it depends on reciprocity and trust to succeed. "Pay what you want" (PWYW) is sometimes used synonymously, but "pay what you can" is often more oriented to charity or socially oriented uses, based more on ability to pay, while "pay what you want" is often more broadly oriented to perceived value in combination with willingness and ability to pay. Examples: E-leiloes, Tecnobid, Pay As You Please, FindBed, Ebay

What is the Business Model Canvas? How can it be used for growth?

The Business Model Canvas is not a Business Model itself but rather a tool to evaluate, improve end eventually generate a specific business model. It is a very useful tool for explaining the relevant variables that must be considered when developing a business model. The principal obvious limitation of this tool is that it is mostly qualitative and when numbers or quantitative information are gathered, some ideas might be not appropriate, balanced or consistent. It a very good tool for teaching and a very good tool for improving an existing business when quantitative information is available and considered in the process.

The Business Model Canvas makes a major contribution to the tools used for business model generation teaching and business model improvement. This model shows a very logical way of considering a business where we have the Inputs, the Outputs and the transformation process (value proposition). The logics used in the Business Model Canvas is based on a balance sheet. The strong logics behind the tool and the visual synthesis are the main reasons for its wide success (see The BCR, Vol. 2, for more information on this).

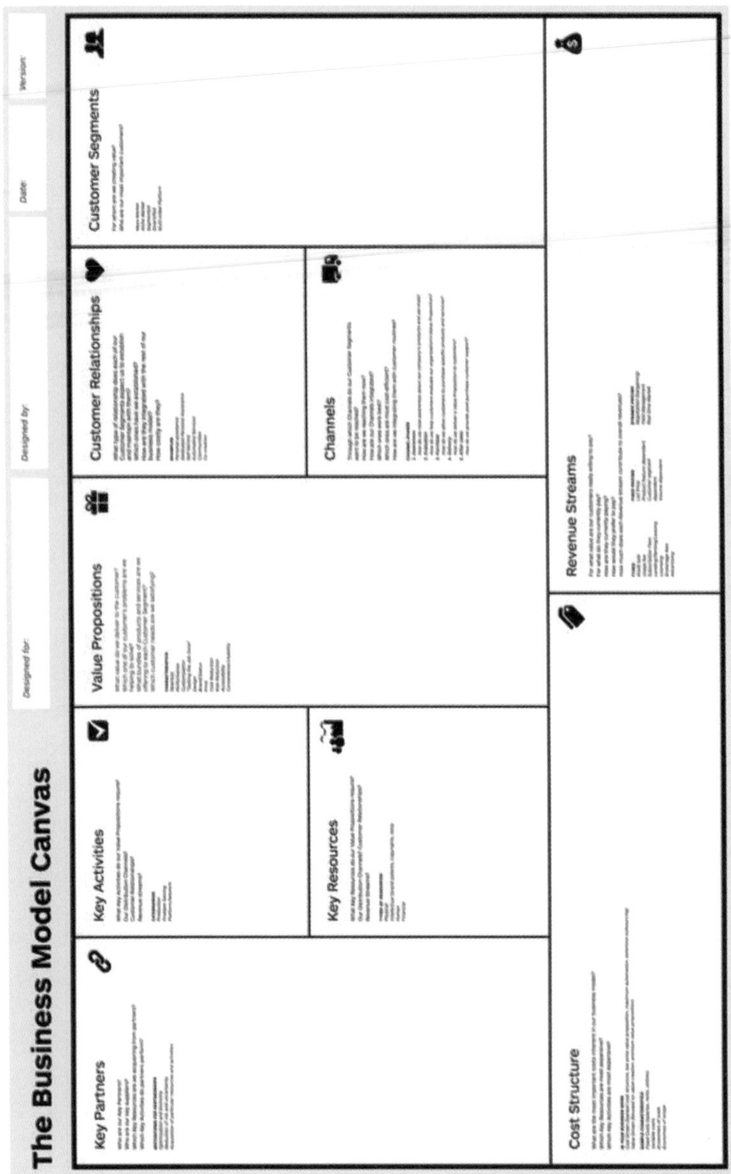

Source: Osterwalder et al. (2010), retrieved from https://en.wikipedia.org/wiki/Business_Model_Canvas, in 29/8/2019.

The 'business model is comparable to the process of 'how to fish'...

> **GIVE A MAN A FISH AND YOU FEED HIM FOR A DAY. TEACH A MAN TO FISH AND YOU FEED HIM FOR A LIFETIME.**
>
> - FISH = INFORMATION -
>
> - TEACH = KNOWLEDGE -

KEY IDEAS AND REFERENCES FOR MORE INFORMATION

- Business models are a critical part of the Business Case Roadmap as they define the nature of the business process
- There are many possible business models and it is possible - and advisable - to combine them
- Knowledge of the business model is very important both when designing a business and when improving it

[1] Osterwalder, A., Pigneur, Y. and Smith, A. (2010) Business Model Generation, John Wiley & Sons, New Jersey.

[2] Kaplan, S. (2012) The Business Model Innovation Factory: How to Stay Relevant When The World is Changing, John Wiley & Sons, New Jersey.

[3] Linz, C., Müller-Stewens, G. and Zimmermann, A. (2017) Radical Business Model Transformation: Gaining the Competitive Edge in a Disruptive World, Kogan Page Limited, New York.

[4] Linz, C., Müller-Stewens, G. and Zimmermann, A. (2020) Radical Business Model Transformation: How Leading Organizations Have Successfully Adapted to Disruption. Kogan Page Limited, New York.in press.

[5] Caudron, J. and Van Peteghem, D. (2018) Digital Transformation: a model to master digital disruption, 3rd edition, Bookbaby.

15

What are the drivers for the International Marketing Plan?

Why is the international marketing plan critical for growth?

Marketing and communication are - alongside leadership, and infrastructure development - one of the three main challenges for growth. In fact, one of the key success factors for business expansion is the international vision and approach for business development. An international marketing plan is a marketing plan aimed at global expansion of product sales and brand recognition. International marketing is aimed at deciding the right dose of tailoring or standardising products or services, marketing, and sales tactics to suit the international market the company is expanding into. It involves the work of deciding on the standardisation vs. adaptation dilemma, at all levels of marketing, from value proposition through to communication.

Why does growth usually require an international evolution?

Fast growing companies usually have an international perspective right from the get-go. Others take that direction after initially starting their operations locally. Often, local, regional or national markets are too small for a specific product or service. This is specifically true for SMEs of small open economies. Even firms from large domestic markets need to consider international expansion in order to keep up with the objective of growth.

How can an international marketing plan be developed?

There are a number of elements in the international marketing plan. These should include: an expression of the stakeholders' expectations; an audit of the firm's strengths, weaknesses and future potential capabilities; an assessment of the likely changes in the external environment and the opportunities and threats which will result; a statement of corporate objectives; an evaluation of possible strategic options; an assessment of likely competitor responses to the strategic options; and the selection and justification of the appropriate strategy.

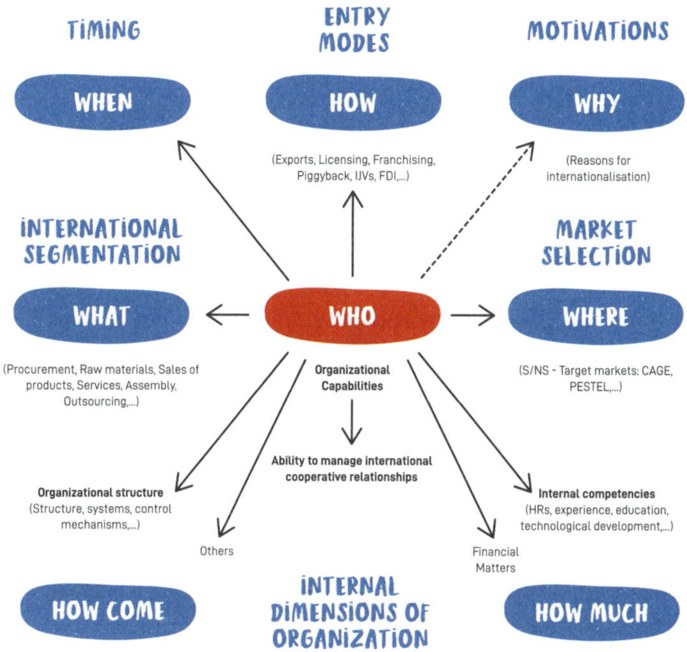

Source: adapted from Silva et al. (2018) Marketing Internacional, Actual.

What is the most frequent pattern followed in internationalisation?

Frequently, companies that do not start as international, begin their operations at home and then expand incrementally and gradually to geographically closer markets. They do so using gradually heavier entry modes and serving first fewer, and then increasingly more, target markets. This traditional pattern of internationalisation is depicted below and is known as the "Uppsala Model".

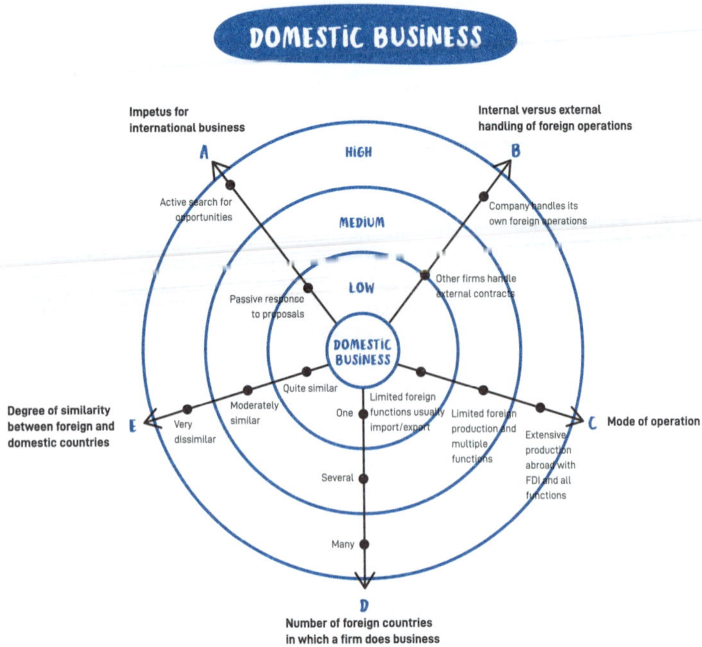

Source: adapted from Daniels, Radebaugh and Sullivan (2015).

What is the difference between International, Multi-national and Trans-national?

There are different possibilities for the way a firm's international marketing activities are organised. Hence, it is important to understand the different types of international business strategy. This is especially important to develop partnerships.

1. **International companies** are normally companies that extend their activities outside the scope of their original market. They do not normally invest outside of their home country, but they are international because the context in which they are dealing is international.
2. **Multinational companies** have locations or facilities in multiple countries, but each location functions in its own way, essentially as an independent entity. Multinational companies have investment in other countries, but do not have coordinated product offerings in each country. These firms are more focused on adapting their products and services to each individual local market.
3. **Transnational companies** are complex organisations that substantial facilities, do business in more than one country and do not consider any particular country as their national home. One of the significant advantages of a transnational company is that they are able to maintain a greater degree of responsiveness to the local markets where they maintain facilities. Transnational companies are much more complex organisations. They have invested in foreign operations, have a central corporate facility but give decision-making, R&D and marketing powers to each individual foreign market.

What is a metanational company?

Metanational companies operate to a new paradigm. They do not derive their competitive advantage from their home country, or from a set of national subsidiaries. Metanationals view the world as a global canvas dotted with pockets of technology, market intelligence, and capabilities. They see untapped potential in these pockets of specialist knowledge scattered around the world. By sensing and mobilising this scattered knowledge, they are able to innovate more effectively than their rivals are.

KEY IDEAS AND REFERENCES FOR MORE INFORMATION

- Marketing - together with Leadership and Infrastructure development - presents one of the three main challenges for growth
- Growth usually requires an international drive and natural evolution path
- Communication through marketing is very important in the marketplace but also internally
- It is very complex to develop an international marketing process over time and within different geographies

[1] Doz ,Y. and Santos, J. (2001) From Global to Metanational: How Companies Win in the Knowledge Economy, Harvard Business Review Press.

[2] Stonehouse, G., Campbell, D., Hamill, J. and Purdie, T. (2004) Global and Transnational Business: Strategy and Management, Wiley.

[3] Hollensen, S. (2016), Global Marketing, 7th ed., Pearson.

[4] Silva et al. (2018) Marketing Internacional, Actual, Coimbra.

16

How can exports be combined with international business development?

What is the relevance of going international for business growth?

Companies go international for one of three basic reasons: pro-active reasons, reactive reasons, and reasons that combine the two. In essence, reactive reasons are associated with the imperatives of the business (for example, demolition or aviation companies that need to operate in a global way) and reasons that involve following partners (for instance a client enters a new market and requires the supplier firm to follow). Pro-active reasons are basically those motivated by a company's desire to grow or expand operations. More specific motives include generating more revenue, competing for new sales, investment opportunities, diversifying, take advantage of reduced costs and recruiting new talent. Other reasons may include taking advantage of governmental support, country-of-origin effects or economies of scale or scope.

What are the most common mistakes in import/export business?

The simplest way to internationalise is, as we have previously said, through exports. We can summarise import/export mistakes as follows:

Import / export management mistakes
1. Lack of strategy: export requires defining a prior strategy before making decisions
2. Lack of knowledge in import and export regulations. This is mandatory!
3. Hiring an unexperienced customs broker. Customs brokerage is very specialised and specific
4. Not declaring the correct value to customs. This usually results in fines and legal proceedings
5. Unfamiliarity with Incoterms (*)
6. Failing to insure goods. Also lack of protection against currency fluctuations
7. Not verifying the legitimacy of the supplier or buyer of the product through due diligence
8. Appropriate contracts. Sketchy Payment Agreement Terms generate large problems
9. Underestimating competition and expenses
10. Personal relationships

(*) To facilitate commerce around the world, the International Chamber of Commerce (ICC) publishes a set of Incoterms, officially known as international commercial terms.

Why are partnerships critical for international business growth?

There are several key reasons why partnerships are especially important when doing international business.

Reasons for international partnerships
1. Forming economies of scale with partners whenever possible
2. Enhancing competitiveness relating to other companies in the market
3. Dividing risks, mostly at cost level
4. Setting new standards for technology, pulled by a more diverse set of market drivers
5. Entering new markets as a result of a larger geographic coverage
6. Overcoming the competition in a market using partner's strengths

There are decisions to be made at each phase of the JV partnering process.

ASSESSING STRATEGIC RATIONALE	SELECTING A PARTNER	NEGOTIATING TERMS	IMPLEMENTATION AND MANAGEMENT
- What are our objectives? - What sort of resources do we need to achieve our objectives • Do we want to access or acquire these resources? - Are we in this for the long or short term? - Is a Joint Venture (JV) our best option?	- Does the partner have the resources we need? - Will they provide us access to the resources we need? - What are their goals? - Are their goals congruent with ours? - What are their motives? - Are we compatible? - Do they have experience in managing JVs?	- Is our management in full support of the JV? - What is best for the JV? - What is the relative importance of each of our requirements? - What are the typical practices in the industry/country in which the JV is located? - How should the performance of the JV be assessed? - Is each party aware of the other's assumptions? - What level of equity is appropriate? - Who will be responsible for managing the JV? - Are there any unresolved issues?	- How do we handle disputes that may arise? - Are we learning form our JV? - How do we renegotiate terms if one or more partners think it is necessary? - Are we capturing and codifying any JV management capabilities? - If the JV does not perform as anticipated, how do we turn it around? - Under what conditions should we terminate the JV?

Source: adapted from Beamish and Lupton (2009).

What are the different decisions that can be made at an international marketing level?

A major concern for managers deciding on a global business strategy is the tradeoff between global integration and local responsiveness. Global integration is the degree to which the company is able to use the same products and methods in other countries. Local responsiveness is the degree to which the company must customise its products and methods to meet conditions in other countries. The two dimensions result in four basic global business strategies: export, standardisation, multi-domestic, and transnational. These are shown in the figure below.

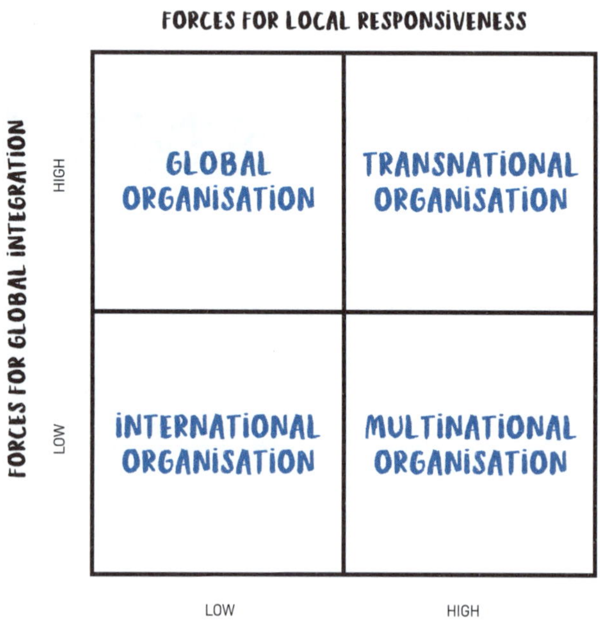

Source: adapted from Bartlett & Ghoshal (1989), p. 438.

KEY IDEAS AND REFERENCES FOR MORE INFORMATION

- Exports are one form of international business. International trade is very relevant for business growth
- Alternatively the company may consider the possibility of establishing a partnership that has two basic purposes: strengthening a firm's competitiveness by partnering with someone alike, or improving its competencies in a complementary way with a different partner
- The development of a growth strategy for business requires knowledge about the possible alternative ways of generating value by analysing opportunities and possible partnerships worldwide

[1] Helpman, E. (2011) Understanding Global Trade. Harvard University Press, Belknap Press.

[2] Capela, J. J. (2015) Import / Export Kit For Dummies, 3rd ed., For Dummies

[3] Silva et al (2018) Marketing Internacional, Actual, Coimbra.

17

How can we use 'value chain analysis' for business development?

What is the 'value chain'? What is its relevance for growth?

A value chain is a set of activities that a firm operating in a specific industry performs in order to deliver a valuable product or service to the market. The concept comes from business management and was first described by Michael Porter in his 1985 best-seller: Competitive Advantage: Creating and Sustaining Superior Performance.

It is very important to understand the difference between the business value chain and the product value chain. The development of an operational growth strategy must consider the possibilities brought by the value chain. (See the The BCR Vol. 2, p. 129).

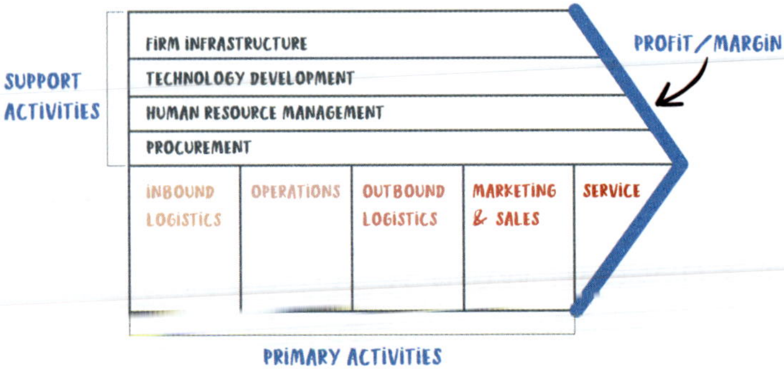

What is a product value chain?

The idea of the value chain is based on the way organisation understands its processes. This involve the idea of seeing a manufacturing (or service) organisation as a system, made up of sub-systems - each with inputs, transformation processes and outputs. Inputs, transformation processes, and outputs involve the acquisition and consumption of resources – money, labour, materials, equipment, buildings, land, administration and management. The way that value chain activities are carried out determines costs and affects profits.

The product value chain represents the different sub-products that can be obtained from a specific product. For example, from milk, we can produce butter, cheese and yoghurts, and from the refining of crude oil we can obtain petrol, diesel and aromatic products.

What is the business value chain?

Understanding the business value chain requires the understanding of different perspectives that characterise the value chain. The supply chain is where value is developed and is the backbone of the value chain.

A supply chain represents the steps required in order to get the product or service to the customer. While a supply chain involves all parties in the fulfilment of a customer's request - and ultimately, in customer satisfaction - a value chain is a set of interrelated activities a company uses to create a competitive advantage.
The supply chain is the end-to-end connection of all the parties, resources, businesses and activities involved in the marketing or distribution through which a product reaches its end user. It creates a link between the channel partners like suppliers, manufacturers, wholesalers, distributors, retailers, and the customer. To put simply, it encompasses the flow and storage of the raw material; semi-finished goods and the finished goods from point of origin to final destination, i.e. consumption.
A supply chain refers to the integration of all activities involved in sourcing, procurement, conversion and logistics. On the other hand, value chain implies the series of business operations in which utility is added to the goods and services offered by the firm so as to enhance customer value.
The supply chain is the interconnection of all functions, starting from the manufacturing of raw material into the finished product, and ending when the product reaches the final customer. The value chain, on the other hand, is a set of activities that focuses on creating or adding value to the product.

A good example of the business value chain is the set of processes from farm to fork, in which an agricultural product goes through a set of stages and transformations until it reaches the dish of the final consumer.

What are value and margin?

Value is the total amount (i.e. total revenue) that buyers are willing to pay for a firm's product. The difference between the total value and the total cost of performing all of the firm's activities provides the margin.

Margin implies that organisations realise a profit margin that is dependent on their ability to manage the linkages between all activities in the value chain. In other words, the organisation is able to deliver a product or service, for which the customer is willing to pay more than the sum of the costs of all activities in the value chain.

What is the value chain analysis?

A value chain concentrates on the activities that begin with raw materials, right up to their conversion into the final goods or services. The sources of the competitive advantage of a firm can be seen from its discrete activities and how they interact with one another. The ultimate goals in performing value chain analysis are to maximise value creation while also monitoring and minimising costs.

Value chain analysis is a way to visually analyse a company's business activities to see how the company can create a competitive advantage for itself. Value chain analysis helps a company understands how it adds value to something and subsequently how it can sell its product or service for more than the cost of adding the value, thereby generating a profit margin. In other words, if they are run efficiently the value obtained should exceed the costs of running them i.e. customers should return to the organisation and transact freely and willingly.

The understanding of the value chain
Primary Activities: The functions that are directly concerned with the conversion of input into output and distribution activities are called primary activities. They include:
Inbound Logistics: A range of activities such as receiving, storing, distributing, etc., which make goods and services available for operational processes. Some of those activities are material handling, transportation, stock control, etc.
Operations: The activity of transforming input raw material to final product ready for sale, is known as the operation. Machining, assembling and packaging are activities covered under operations.
Outbound Logistics: As the name suggests, these are the activities that help in collecting, storing and delivering the product to the customer.
Marketing and Sales: All activities like advertising, promotion, sales, marketing research, public relations, etc. which are performed in order to make the customer aware of the product or service and create demand for it, come under marketing.
Service: This means the service provided to the customer so as to improve or maintain the value of the product. It includes financing service, after-sales service and so on.
Support Activities: Those activities, which assist in the accomplishment of primary activities, are support activities. These are:
Procurement: This activity serves the organisation, by supplying all the necessary inputs like material, machinery or other consumable items that are required by the organisation for performing primary activities.
Technology Development: At present, technology development requires heavy investment and years of research and development. However, its benefits can be enjoyed for several years and by a multitude of users in the organisation.
Human Resource Management: This is the most common and important activity of all the primary activities of the organisation. It encompasses overseeing the selection, retention, promotion, transfer, appraisal and dismissal of staff.
Infrastructure: This is the management system, which provides its services to the whole organisation and includes planning, finance, information management, quality control, legal, government affairs, etc.

Source: adapted from https://businessjargons.com/value-chain-analysis.html, consulted in 27/7/2019.

How can growth be optimised along the value chain?

Best practices show that a business's growth strategy can benefit from including detailed knowledge about the related value chain. This is very important because suppliers, clients and competitors do not present the only avenues for growth. Often, partnerships or acquisitions throughout the value chain can be relevant for business growth. This is the case in most mergers and acquisitions.

The value chain is no longer a linear process. Cross-sectorial collaboration, innovation and entrepreneurship development along the value chain are increasingly changing them. They are not linear and static anymore.

KEY IDEAS AND REFERENCES FOR MORE INFORMATION

- The value chain is a unique tool for business growth development
- Business value chains and product value chains must be considered in business formulation
- Business value chain analysis is an essential process for international business

[1] 50Minutes (2015) Michael Porter's Value Chain: Unlock your company's competitive advantage
[2] Culbreth, D. N. (2017) Dynamic Value Chains: Visualizing and Optimizing Your Business, Business Visualization and Optimization.
[3] Chopra, S. and Meindl, P. (2004) Supply Chain Management: Strategy, Planning, and Operation, Prentice Hall.
[4] Arthur, B. (2011) The Nature of Technology: What It Is and How It Evolves~, Penguin Group.
[5] Gaule, A. (000) Purpose to Performance: Innovative New Value Chains, Gallery Books.
[6] Di, C., & Yu, F. (2012). Enterprise Mergers and Acquisitions in the Light of the Value Chain Optimization. In Advances in Computer Science and Engineering (pp. 185-191). Springer, Berlin, Heidelberg.

18

What are the main challenges for a developing business?

What are the barriers to growth?

Growth is very important, as is evident from the different views of business life cycles (see The BCR, Vol. 1). Growing businesses face a range of challenges. As a business grows, different problems and opportunities demand different solutions; what worked a year ago might be not the best approach now. An understanding of the main barriers for business growth may allow growing business to pay special attention to these factors and pre-emptively manage them. As we have already mentioned, there are three main obstacles.

Leadership	Infrastructure	Communication
Leadership development across all levels of the organisation.	Infrastructure development and scalability	Marketing and all related tools are critical both internally and externally

What are the challenges for growth?

Different organisations respond to growth barriers in different ways. A synthesis of the main challenges described in literature can be summarised as follows:

Planning ahead The plan that made sense for you a year ago is not necessarily right for you now. Market conditions continually change, so you need to revisit and update your business plan regularly.
Keeping up with the market Business conditions change continually, so your market research should be continuous as well. Market research is not something you do as a one-off when you launch your business.
Cash flow and financial management Good cash flow control is important for any business. Cash constraints can be the biggest factor limiting growth, and overtrading can be fatal.
Skills and attitudes Entrepreneurs are the driving force behind creating and growing new businesses. All too often, they are also the people holding them back.
The right systems All businesses produce and rely on large volumes of information: financial records, interactions with customers and other business contacts, employee details, regulatory requirements and so on. It is not possible to effectively keep track of them without the right systems.
Welcoming change Complacency can be a major threat to a growing business. Assuming that you will continue to be successful simply because you have been in the past is very unwise.
Problem solving New businesses often run in perpetual crisis mode. Every day brings new challenges that urgently need resolving and management spends most of their time troubleshooting.

What is the role of motivation in business growth?

The importance of motivation in business should not be underestimated. The process of motivation plays a very important role in any organisation, profit or non-profit.

Motivation as a process leads to an increase in employees' productivity. Motivation meets the needs of the employee and thereby creates the drive to work at the best of his or her abilities.

Some best practices to increase motivation include:

- Continuing to develop employees through consistent training.
- Always promoting from within to make sure all staff members know that progression is possible - or likely - in their future within the organisation.
- Tracking performance metrics to keep employees performing well and knowing what improvements need to be made so they stay in line with company goals.

What is Theory X and Theory Y?

In 1960, Douglas McGregor formulated Theory X and Theory Y, suggesting two aspects of human behaviour in the workplace - or, alternatively, two different ways of viewing individuals (employees): one of them negative (Theory X), and the other positive (Theory Y). According to McGregor, managers' perception of the nature of individuals is based on various assumptions. These 'theories' became reference concepts associated with motivation drivers in developing businesses.

Assumptions of Theory X

An average employee intrinsically does not like work and tries to escape it whenever possible.

Since the employee does not want to work, he must be persuaded, compelled, or warned with punishment so as to achieve the organisation's goals. A close degree of supervision by managers is required. The managers adopt a more dictatorial style.

Many employees rank job security as their top priority, and have little or no aspiration/ambition.

Employees generally dislike responsibilities.

Employees resist change.

An average employee needs formal direction

Assumptions of Theory Y

Employees can perceive their job as being relaxing and normal.

They exercise physical and mental effort at work as a matter of course.

Employees may not require only threat, external control and coercion to work, but can use self-direction and self-control if they are dedicated and sincere in their pursuit of the organisation's objectives.

If the job is rewarding and satisfying, it will result in employees' loyalty and commitment to the organisation.

Douglas Murray McGregor (1906 – 1 October 1964) was a management professor at the MIT Sloan School of Management and president of Antioch College from 1948 to 1954.[1] He also taught at the Indian Institute of Management Calcutta. His 1960 book The Human Side of Enterprise had a profound influence on education practices.

Douglas McGregor is a contemporary of Abraham Maslow. Likewise, he also contributed much to the development of the management and motivational theory. He is best known for his Theory X and Theory Y as presented in his book 'The Human Side of Enterprise' (1960), which proposed that a manager's individual assumptions about human nature and behaviour determine how that person manages their employees.

What is Theory Z?

Theory Z is a name for various theories of human motivation, following on from Douglas McGregor's Theory X and Theory Y. According to William Ouchi, Theory Z management tends to promote stable employment, high productivity, and high employee morale and satisfaction. For Ouchi, Theory Z (1981) is focused on increasing an employee's loyalty to the company by providing a job for life with a strong focus on his or her well-being, both on and off the job.

What are the signs of growing pains?

Growth is usually silent for leaders and top managers; very often they do not realise the growing pains the organisation is feeling. Therefore, it is important to recognise the symptoms, so as to be able to initiate potential 'remedies' as soon as possible and mitigate the impacts. An analysis of the views of different experts allows us to bring together the following statements:

Signs of growing pains: symptoms
1. Too Little Time When employees start to feel like there is never enough time to accomplish necessary tasks.
2. Constantly Putting Out Fires When staff are repeatedly spending time dealing with short-term crises, it is often because of a lack of long-range / strategic planning.
3. Lack of Direction This is closely related to the issue of employees constantly putting out fires, and the solution, again, is strategic planning.
4. Working in a Bubble When employees are unaware of the exact nature of their jobs and how they relate to those of others.

5. Too Few Good Managers A business may have a significant number of people who hold the title of "manager," but it may not have many good managers.
6. Unproductive Meetings It is problematic when meetings become a waste of time.

Growing pains: the pathologies
1. Burnout - physical, mental, and emotional.
2. Ad hoc Planning - the type of planning which involves "putting out fires" and handling the "squeaky wheel".
3. Overly optimistic - commonly referred to as "unrealistic". Related to setting improbable expectations and goals.
4. Poor cash flow - when the money runs out before the end of the month.
5. Underpricing - pricing below what is needed to keep you in business.
6. Underarming - the evil twin of underpricing.
7. Poor system development - systems developed "as needed" or when current talent leaves your business.
8. Undefined roles - even "me, myself, and I" are uncertain of the next best steps.
9. Inadequate funding - what your parents aptly described as "trying to get blood from a stone."
10. Missed opportunities - what happens while you're dealing with the "growing pains" listed above.

Source: adapted from https://callcap.com/blog/can-a-call-measurement-company-help-ease-growing-pains/, consulted in 30/8/2019.

KEY IDEAS AND REFERENCES FOR MORE INFORMATION

- There are 3 main barriers to business growth: leadership, infrastructures and communication
- Motivation is definitively a key driver for growth
- The management of growing pains can significantly smooth the growing process.

[1] Barrier to Growth,The Growth Institute, www.growthinstitute.com

[2] Chesbrough, H. (2006) Open Innovation: The New Imperative for Creating and Profiting from Technology, Harvard Business Review Press.

[3] Info Entrepreneurs (2009), The challenges of growing a business - and how to meet them, Business Link UK

[4] McGregor, D. (2006) The Human Side of Enterprise, Annotated Edition, McGraw-Hill Education

19

What are the main business management and business strategy mistakes?

Why is business strategy important for growth?

Growth will not happen without an implicit or explicit business strategy. Growth may be an objective, and strategy will define the path to get there; it will allow existing barriers to be overcome, and will help avoid common mistakes. Leadership should involve all stakeholders in strategy decisions.

What is business strategy?

A business strategy is a set of competitive moves and actions that a business uses to attract customers, compete successfully, strengthen performance, and achieve organisational goals. It outlines how business should be carried out to reach the desired ends. Business strategy can be understood as being the course of action or set of decisions, which assists the entrepreneurs in achieving specific business objectives. It is simply a 'master plan' that the management of a company implements to secure a competitive position in the market, carry on its operations, please customers and achieve the desired aims of the business. (For detailed information on this topic, see The BCR Vol. 3, chapter 2).

Business strategy levels
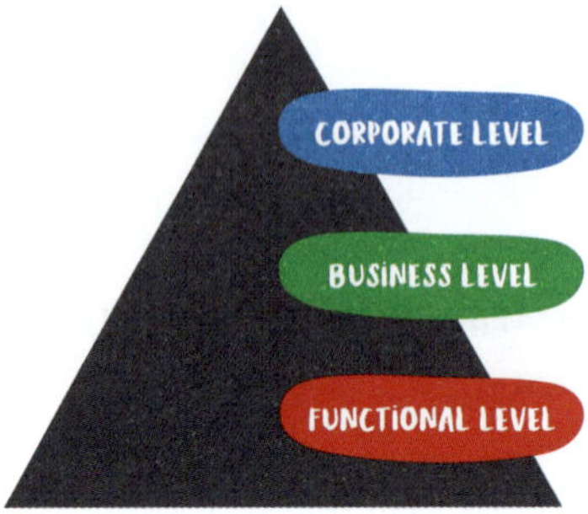
Corporate level strategy: Corporate level strategy is a long-range, action-oriented, integrated and comprehensive plan formulated by the top management. It is used to ascertain business lines, expansion and growth, takeovers and mergers, diversification, integration, new areas for investment and divestment and so forth.
Business level strategy: The strategies that relate to a particular business are known as business level strategies. These are developed by the general managers, who convert mission and vision into concrete strategies. They are like blueprints for the entire business.
Functional level strategy: Developed by first line managers or supervisors, functional level strategy involves decision-making at the operational level concerning particular functional areas like marketing, production, human resource, research and development, finance and so on.

What is a management mistake?

Generally, a mistake is a decision or an action that we come to regret. Mistakes usually cause some degree of pain, loss or struggle. However, these events that we try so hard to avoid, may be precisely what we need in order to become experienced. Mistakes represent a misunderstanding or erroneous belief about a material fact, which may prevent the formation of a valid contract. There are three basic types:

(1) Common mistake: all parties make the same error.
(2) Mutual mistake: all parties are mistaken or fail to understand each other.
(3) Unilateral mistake: only one party is mistaken.

The first step to avoid and eventually correct mistakes is to understand them.

What are the main business strategy mistakes?

Business strategy mistakes are a special type of mistake. They are often a result of misunderstandings of concepts and ideas. These mistakes are both common and costly. Getting smarter about how competition works and what strategy is will save you from making them.

Business management mistakes
1. Confusing marketing with strategy. A value proposition is not the same thing as a strategy. If you are trying to describe a strategy, the value proposition is a natural place to begin; it is intuitive to think of strategy in terms of the mix of benefits aimed at meeting customers' needs. But, as important as it is to have insight into customers' needs, do not confuse marketing with strategy. What the marketing-only approach misses is that a robust strategy also requires a tailored value chain, a unique configuration of activities that best delivers that kind of value. This element of strategy is not at all intuitive, but it is absolutely essential. If you perform the same activities as everyone else, in the same ways, how can you expect to achieve better performance? To establish a competitive advantage, a company must deliver its distinctive value through a distinctive value chain. It must perform different activities than that of rivals, or perform similar activities in different ways.
2. Confusing competitive advantage with "what you're good at." Building on strengths is a good thing, but when it comes to strategy, companies are too often inward-looking, and therefore likely to overestimate their strengths. You might perceive customer service as a strong area. Therefore, that becomes the "strength" on which you attempt to build a strategy. But a real strength for strategy purposes has to be something the company can do better than any of its rivals. And, "better" because you are choosing to meet different needs and performing different activities than they perform, because you've chosen a different configuration for your value chain than they have.
3. Pursuing size above all else, because if you are the biggest, you will be more profitable. There is at least a grain of truth in this thinking, which is precisely what makes it so dangerous. But, before you assume that bigger is always better, it is critical to run the numbers for your business. Too often, the goal is chosen because it sounds good, whether or not the economics of the business support the logic. In industry after industry, Porter notes that economies of scale are exhausted at a relatively small share of industry sales. There is no systematic evidence that indicates that industry leaders are the most profitable or successful firms. To cite one notorious example, General Motors was the world's largest car company for a period of decades, a fact that did not prevent its descent into bankruptcy. To the extent that size mattered at all, it might be more accurate to say that GM was too big to succeed. Meanwhile, BMW, small by industry standards, has a history of superior returns. Over the past decade (2000-2009), its average return on invested capital was 50 percent higher than the industry average. Companies only have to be "big enough," which rarely means they have to dominate. Often "big enough" is just 10 percent of the market.
4. Thinking that "growth" or "reaching $1 billion in revenue" is a strategy. Do not confuse strategy with actions (growing, acquiring, divesting, etc.) or with goals, (reaching X billion in sales, or Y share of the market). Porter's definition is that it is the set of integrated choices that define how you will achieve superior performance in the face of competition. It is not the goal (e.g. being number one or reaching $1 billion in top-line revenue), nor is it a specific action (e.g., making acquisitions). It is the positioning you choose that will result in achieving the goal; the actions are the path you take to realise the positioning. Moreover, when Porter defines strategy, he is really talking about what constitutes a good strategy - one that will result in a higher ROIC than the industry average. The real problem here is that you might think you have a strategy when you do not.

5. Focusing on high-growth markets, because that is where the money is.
Managers often mistakenly assume that a high-growth industry will be an attractive one. Wrong. Growth is no guarantee that the industry will be profitable. For example, growth might put suppliers in the driving seat, pushing up the industry's costs and limiting profitability. Alternatively, combined with low entry barriers, growth might attract new rivals, thereby increasing competition and driving prices down. Growth alone says nothing about the power of customers or the availability of substitutes, both of which would dampen profitability. The untested assumption that a fast-growing industry is a "good" industry, Porter warns, often leads to bad strategy decisions.

Source: adapted from Joan Magretta (2011) Five Common Strategy Mistakes, Harvard Business Review, Dec.8.

How can we avoid business strategy mistakes?

Some people argue that 60% of strategies fail; others say it's closer to 90%. Either way, the consensus seems clear: most strategies fail.

These are the top 10 reasons most strategies fail
1. Starting too early — strategy was not implemented in the right momentum and the market might have not been ready for it yet
2. Including the wrong people — people who are not aligned with the strategy and the culture of the organisation
3. Not including the right people — failing in getting the right people in the key areas of the company (Ex: HRs, R&D, finance...)
4. A lack of focus — many things attempted at the same time and lack of a specific approach to business
5. A lack of honesty — when the company acts behind the scenes or in grey areas; it normally starts with schemas that are assembled with employees for the company's own benefit
6. Not taking advantage of core competencies — which basically means not fully using the critical resources of the company
7. Resistance to change — this has to do with the difficulties associated with acting outside the comfort area
8. Lack of rigour — not being accurate, confusing information and not describing relevant details
9. Unrealistic goals — setting objectives that are too ambitious or unachievable in the defined timeframe and without consideration of the resources available
10. Lack of accountability — this has to do with the lack of reports and the registration of the costs incurred

Source: adapted from: www.executestrategy.net/blog/why-strategies-fail, consulted in 25/6/2019.

How to fix some mistakes	
Written down	• Capture all your tasks and open loops by writing everything down • Do not worry about organisation or prioritisation first; your mind is for thinking, not remembering
Focus	• Prioritise and stick to three main tasks each day • Do them in order of importance and urgency
Be specific	• Make sure each task is relevant to your goals • Make them specific and measurable
Use time in blocks	• Assign each task to a set timeframe within your day • Avoid multi-tasking and focus on deep work
Having no rest periods	• Schedule rest periods between each task • Take note of the length (how long) and quality (what you do) to maximise each rest period

Source: adapted from www.productiveandfree.com, consulted in 20/6/2019.

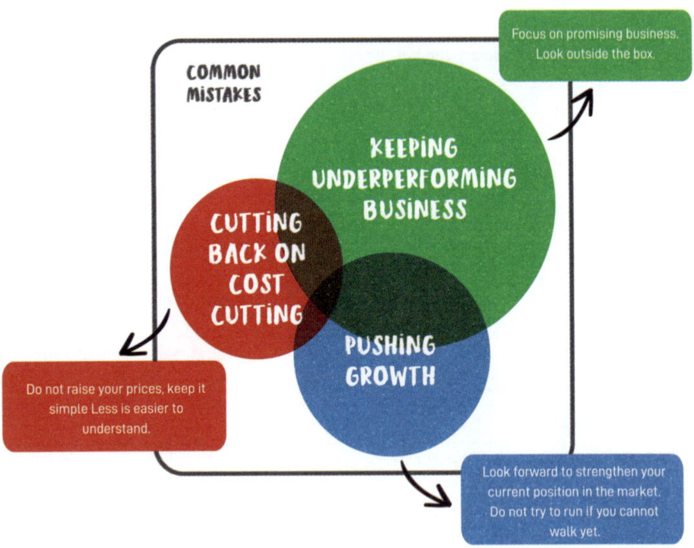

Source: adapted from: https://flevy.com/browse/slideshow/common-mistakes-in-business-strategy-251, consulted in 30/6/2019.

What is the 'business growth paradox'?

This has to do with the (naïve) belief that as we grow the business and as we take on more team members, client, and business systems, things should get easier. The problem is, sometimes they do not. What actually happens is that things get harder and more complicated as they grow - sometimes a great deal more complicated. This is a counterintuitive situation that represents one of the main conceptual mistakes in business development.

Production scale economies are not automatic with growth. Indeed, it is often the case that heavier quality management systems imply redundancies and related costs might result in higher production costs with scale.

In fact, managing one staff member, one product, or one client, is easy. However, when numbers increase, the situation changes: ten staff members, ten products, ten clients, and, suddenly the web of potential relationships becomes massive. This complexity makes growing the business feel like a painful path to take - and acts as an anchor on aspirations of growth. Therefore, it is no surprise that so many business owners simply give up. The pressure that is slowing them down feels greater than the pressure to grow.

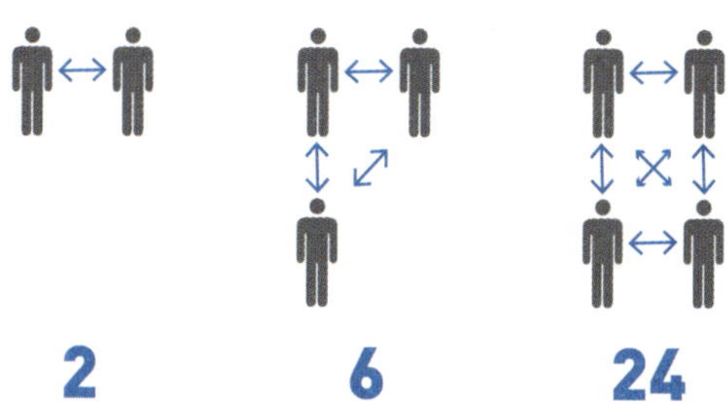

A key component of a differentiated strategy should be its simplicity. Growth creates complexity. Complexity is the silent killer of growth. Complexity just keeps growing exponentially with each person added to the team. This fact explains the barriers to growth, which we referred to previously: leadership, infrastructure development and marketing and communication. With growth, each of these barriers seems progressively harder to overcome. Thus, in many cases, bigger is not always better.

KEY IDEAS AND REFERENCES FOR MORE INFORMATION

- Growth will not happen without strategy, whether implicit or explicit
- It is possible to map and forecast potential mistakes related to business strategy
- A detailed understanding of potential mistakes is the first step in avoiding and managing them if they happen

[1] Gil, E. (2018) High Growth Handbook, Stripe Press.
[2] Rumelt, R. (2011) Good Strategy Bad Strategy: The Difference and Why It Matters, Profile Books.
[3] Kouly, M. (2019) Beyond Strategy: Leading Your Organization To Remarkable Growth, Michael Kouly.
[4] Allio, R. and Fahey, L. (2012) Joan Magretta: what executives can learn from revisiting Michael Porter, Emerald Group Publishing Limited.
[5] Magretta, J. (2011) Understanding Michael Porter: The Essential Guide to Competition and Strategy. Harvard Business Review Press.
[6] Craven, R. (2017) The Business Growth Paradox, https://robert-craven.com/the-business-growth-paradox/.

20

How to sell a business

What are the factors that influence business evaluation?

Business evaluation is very important - not only when selling, but also in buying a business. Business valuation is an estimation of what something is worth, while evaluation is the assessment process. The most appropriate evaluation procedure depends on:

1. The nature and characteristics of the business
2. The prospective buyer
3. The size or scale.

All methods have their strengths and weakness, as well as limits to their applications. The best option is always to combine different evaluation methods in parallel, in order to find a possible convergence. The complexity of business evaluation often requires expert advice or consulting. It is good practice to involve specialist brokers, or consultants when necessary.

Relating to the nature and characteristics of the business, evaluation depends on a wide range of situations but it is possible to define the following decision tree:

Does the business have relevant past performance data available?	Is it a new business which does not yet have historical data?
This is the case of established companies at a tipping point	This is the case for startups or IP-based new companies

For more on this subject, see question number 1 of this volume: What is the 'life cycle' of companies?

It is often the case that new businesses do not have the necessary information regarding their cash-flow - and even more importantly, their activity is based upon intangible assets. Technology start-ups are a good example of these difficulties.

What are intangible assets and how can they be valued?

Intangible assets (intangibles) are long-lived assets used in the production of goods and services. They lack physical properties, instead representing legal rights or competitive advantages (a bundle of rights) developed or acquired by an owner. In order to have value, intangible assets should generate some measurable amount of economic benefit to the owner, such as incremental turnover or earnings (pricing, volume and better delivery, amongst others), cost savings (process economies and marketing cost savings) and increased market share or visibility. Examples include patents, copyrights, or internally developed software, brand names, and customer relations. Before starting the evaluation of intangible assets, there are three questions to ask:

1. What would a willing buyer pay to employ the intangible asset?
2. What is the useful life of this asset?
3. What portion of the operating income does this asset generate?

Methods for evaluation of intangible assets
1. Market Approach Observable (one might say "findable") market-based transactions of identical or substantially similar intangible assets recently exchanged in an arm's length transaction are often difficult to obtain. Publicly-traded data usually represents a market capitalisation of the enterprise, not singular intangible assets. Market data from market participants is often used in income-based models, such as determining reasonable royalty rates and discount rates.
2. Income Approach Income-based models are best used when the intangible asset is income-producing or when it allows an asset to generate cash flow. Just as with other valuation assignments, an income approach technique converts future benefits (such as cash flows or earnings) to a single, discounted amount, usually as a result of increased turnover or cost savings. We have the traditional two choices of either capitalising a single period of benefits or discounting a future stream of benefits.
3. Cost Approach Cost-based analyses are based on the economic principle of substitution and usually ignore the amount, timing and duration of future economic benefits, as well as the risk of performance within a competitive environment. Historical cost reflects only the actual cost that had been incurred to develop the asset. 'Reproduction cost new' implies the current cost of an identical new property. 'Replacement cost new' implies the current cost of a similar new property having the nearest equivalent utility to the property being valued.

Source: proposed by CGMA - Charted Global Management Accountant www.cgma.org, consulted in 30/9/2019.

What are the impacts of intangible assets? How do they differ from tangible assets?

Early in the twenty-first century, the major developed economies began, for the first time, to invest more in intangible assets, like design, branding, R&D, and software, than in tangible assets, like machinery, buildings, and computers. For all sorts of businesses, from tech firms and pharma companies to coffee shops and gyms, the ability to deploy assets that one can neither see nor touch is increasingly the main source of long-term success. These intangible assets have four main characteristics that are very important to understand in order to develop an appropriate valuation and protection strategy:

Sunk Costs	Spillover generator	Scalable nature	Synergies generation
Refers to the fact that intangible investment often has little or no salvage value. Plants and equipment are marketable goods, and in the event that a business fails it can sell those goods in order to provide investors with some compensation.	Refers to the fact that the value of intangible investment can easily be captured by other firms. Ideas can be copied and designs may be "reverse-engineered" by competitors.	Refers to the fact that the intangible value of a brand or idea can be extended at very low marginal cost.	Refers to the fact that the value of a combination of intangible assets cannot be deconstructed into individual components. A successful smart phone incorporates many innovations. Evaluated separately, none of these innovations represents a marketable product.

Source: adapted from: www.econlib.org/library/Columns/y2018/Klingintangible.html consulted in 28/7/2019.

What methods can be used to evaluate a business?

There are three types of methods for all businesses, depending on the information that is available, and the type of business. These methods can be used separately, or combined.

<table>
<tr><th>Objective methods</th><th>Subjective methods</th><th>Comparative methods</th></tr>
<tr><td>Book value
(total assets minus total liabilities)
Discounted Cash Flows
Return on Investment
Cost to re-build</td><td>Real Option Valuation
(common when involves Intellectual Property)
Goodwill
Capitalisation of Earnings
Intangible asset valuation</td><td>EBITDA x multiplier
(when industry multipliers exist)
Multiples of Earnings
Market value
Broker information</td></tr>
<tr><td colspan="3">There are many sources of information about each evaluation method, and experts who are able to provide support. However it is good practice for the interested parties to know the meaning and details of each evaluation method. Typically businesses that rely on intangible assets are more difficult to evaluate — as is the case where intellectual property is concerned.</td></tr>
<tr><td colspan="3">Asset Valuation
Business assets are all the things the business owns that have a value and can be shown on the balance sheet. Assets include land and buildings, equipment and vehicles, cash, supplies, and accounts receivable. Intangible assets like intellectual property also have a value. Selling the entire business based on asset valuation does not usually take into account goodwill.
Goodwill is basically the intangible value of your customer and or knowledge base. From an accounting standpoint it is the premium paid for the business over the book value of the listed assets on the business balance sheet. Intangible assets bring substantial difficulty to the evaluation process, and it is necessary to employ more than basic accounting skills.</td></tr>
<tr><td colspan="3">Cash Flow and Gross Sales
Buyers often want to know how much cash their business can potentially generate. This method uses information from a cash flow statement, showing the inflows and outflows of cash for the business over a specific period of time. Then, this current cash flow figure is discounted for its future subjective value. Multiples of gross sales for the three previous years might be used.</td></tr>
<tr><td colspan="3">Multiples of Earnings
For businesses that have shareholders, looking at multiples of earnings per share of stock is a common valuation method. This number shows the earnings of each shareholder, or EPS, which is not the same as any dividends: First earnings (otherwise known as profits or net income) are determined. Most often, the "raw" earnings number is reduced further, usually by taking out interest and taxes (called EBIT or Earnings Before Interest and Taxes) or the EBITDA (Earnings Before Interest, Taxes, Depreciation, and Amortisation).</td></tr>
</table>

Source: adapted from http://macabacus.com/learn,consulted in 20/7/2019.

What is EBITDA and where to find "multiples"?

EBITDA is one of many complex valuation formulae commonly used in business sales. It is an abbreviation of Earnings Before Interest, Taxes, Depreciation, and Amortisation. EBITDA attempts to measure free cash flow based on the numbers in a company's income and cash flow statements. But like most valuation methods, the effectiveness of EBITDA varies by calculation method and company.

EBITDA equals revenue minus expenses. Interest and taxes, which can vary by situation, are also left out of the equation. Multiples of EBITDA (usually enterprise value divided by EBITDA value) are often used to measure accounting value against market value. In theory, multiples allow buyers to make more accurate apples-to-apples comparisons between businesses. An analyst using the valuation approach assumes that a particular ratio is applicable and applies to various companies operating within the same line of business or industry. In other words, the idea behind the multiples analysis is that when firms are comparable, the multiples approach can be used to determine the value of one firm based on the value of another. The multiples approach seeks to capture many of a firm's operating and financial characteristics (e.g., expected growth) in a single number that can be multiplied by a specific financial metric (e.g., EBITDA) to yield an enterprise or equity value.

Valuation multiples by industry are difficult to obtain, and result from the comparative analysis of many companies in a specific sector, in a specific region, during a specific timeframe. Some possible sources that can be used are: www.epsilon-research.com; www.duffandphelps.com; www.statista.com;

www.mondaq.com; www.eval.tech; www.equidam.com; www.bvresources.com.

What are the main challenges in business evaluation?

Often, the best valuation is a mix of several methods tailored to suit a particular business. This is because business valuation methods are rarely accurate, and the only true valuation is the one agreed upon between the buyer and the seller, after negotiation and the disclosure of comprehensive information. The determination of the value of a business is, in the end, only realised when a willing buyer and willing seller sit down and come to an agreement, and put that agreement in writing. The more valuation methods used, the higher the chance of arriving at a figure. The more figures it is possible to gather, the better the estimate. The business valuation that results from the evaluation methods used is limited by several factors that must be understood when considering the process of selling or buying businesses.

Most business valuations are unrealistic because they do not consider outside or intangible factors. The condition of the economy affects all businesses in many ways, and local economies may have an even greater effect on a business. The timing or momentum associated with the business evaluation and prospective transaction can strongly influence the value, based on the impact of the economic framework on the specific business. This is also true of location, market and technological factors.

What are the most relevant timing considerations for selling?

The time for buying or selling a business is critical. There is a window of opportunity, which can be very wide and always open – or, as is usually the case, open for just a very short period. Market valuation and readiness to sell are two possible criteria to consider in relation to the opportunity to sell. They can be described as follows.

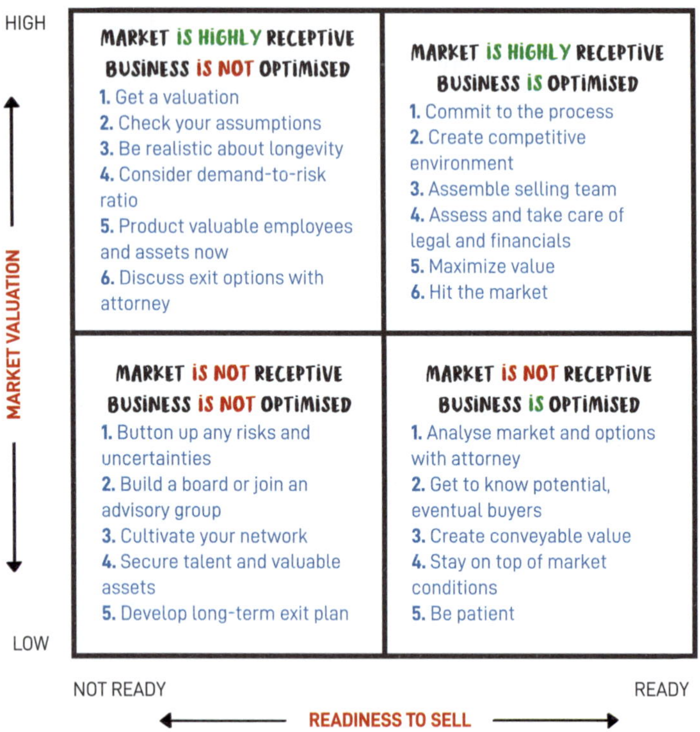

Source: adapted from: www.offitkurman.com, accessed in 21/7/2019.

When and why to sell a business?

The process of selling a business typically takes 6 to 9 months (depending on the nature of business), but for planning purposes, a year should be a good timescale when considering selling. It is very good practice to plan to sell or buy in advance, so that a proper evaluation is conducted and the most important uncertainties are known and worked out using a risk management approach. To know the most frequent reasons for the sale of a business is important, for both buyers and sellers, if they want to find opportunities.

What are the top 10 reasons why small businesses change hands?
1. A primary owner dies unexpectedly. The owner — who was not considering transitioning the ownership of his or her business — passes away. We might ask a few questions here: To whom does ownership pass? Is there a buy-sell agreement that will dictate the pricing and terms of the ownership sale? Is life insurance in place to fund the purchase of this owner's shares? Are there appropriate plans in place to assure a smooth transition, not only of ownership, but of management, as well? These are things to think about while we are still alive. Otherwise, families, fellow owners, key employees and others are left to sort things out, under often unfavourable and difficult circumstances.
2. A key employee leaves. The departure of an employee can trigger the necessity to sell the entire business under unfavourable circumstances. This might be particularly true if this key person takes with them important contacts, critical energy, and/or leadership that keep things going and growing. A couple of questions to ask include: Does the business have such an employee or employees? Are they owners of businesses subject to buy-sell agreements and/or employee agreements, if appropriate?
3. The owner gets "tired" and decides to sell. This is an unbelievably frequent reason why business ownership transfers occur. This circumstance might happen with small businesses, but also with larger ones. However, it is important to note that if a business owner waits until he feels "tired," this is already a sign that the business is on the downside of the life cycle curve. Tired owners almost unavoidably transmit their "tiredness" to employees and customers in many subtle ways. In the process, their businesses may lose the vital force that is critical for ongoing growth and success.
4. Unexpected offers come along. Occasionally, business owners receive unexpected offers to purchase the businesses. When this occurs for a particular owner, he/she sometimes sell to the surprise bidder, or decides then to put the company "in play" and sell to another, higher bidder. The questions here are: Is the business ready to be marketed? Is the owner ready for a transaction with his or her personal planning in place? Is the stock of the business distributed to family or other employees such that others could benefit appropriately? Just because someone comes along with a good price, even an outrageous price, does not mean that the time is ready for ownership transition and sale.

5. Business reversals happen. Perhaps a company fails to adapt to changing markets, competition arises from unexpected quarters, or an accident or bad luck generates substantial losses. Sometimes the affected business never recovers and a forced sale is the result. This is obviously not a desirable outcome. This happens when a business is not able to react and adapt to sudden changes in the market.
6. The primary owner divorces. Marital dissolutions where closely held or family businesses are substantial marital assets occur with increasing frequency. Wild card divorce judgements can create settlement terms that are so onerous that a business needs to be sold to settle the marital estate. Emotional changes resulting from the divorce can also create the necessity or the desire to sell the business. Often one party is not able to gain control and business brokers are called in to sell the business.
7. Life-changing experiences occur. Business owners sometimes encounter life-changing experiences such as heart attacks, cancer, or close calls with death in accidents. We all experience the deaths of parents, spouses, and friends. Such events can trigger significant changes in the desire to own and to manage a business. The emotional or physical shock of such experiences sometimes fosters a strong desire to "do things differently with the rest of my life". Business transfers can be the eventual results of these or other life-changing experiences.
8. Gift and estate tax planning. Owners of many successful, closely-held and family businesses engage in gift/donation and estate tax planning as a normal means of ownership transfer. Interestingly, the absence of proper gift and estate tax planning can precipitate the forced sale of a business if an owner's estate lacks the liquidity to handle estate taxes, or if a failure to plan for orderly and qualified management succession cripples the business when the owner is no longer there.
9. The second (or third) generation is not up to the task. There is substantial research indicating that most businesses do not survive to a second generation of family ownership. It is very common that family businesses are not able to set up a professional governance model that sets up a corporate DNA able to survive different generations.
10. Normal lifetime planning dictates timing. Businesses sell as a result of normal lifetime planning by their owners. These owners plan for and execute the sales of their businesses on their own timetable and terms. Numerous transfer mechanisms are employed in such transfers, including management buyouts (MBOs), Employee Stock Ownership Plans (ESOPs), leveraged recapitalisations, and other corporate finance techniques that are used to facilitate ownership transfer, in addition to outright sales. Quite often, such transfers occur over time while ownership and management are transferred in an orderly fashion.

Large companies may follow a different logic - usually related to either growth or survival strategies. See: 01. What is the 'life cycle' of companies? Why is it important for growth?

What are the necessary steps in selling a business?

There are many complex steps in selling a business if it is the result of a structured decision. Many business sales are based on impulsive and emotionally-biased processes, either by the buyers, sellers, or both. The most usual steps for a business sale can be developed via a structured process. A Confidential Business Review, sometimes referred to as Sales Memorandum or simply, "the book", is one of the key communication documents to be prepared for your business by you or your business brokers. It provides comprehensive information about the business to prospective buyers who have signed a non-disclosure agreement.

1. Planning	2. Search	3. Deal-making	4. Closing
First meeting / Desire for info about the selling process	Activate buyer Develop search plan	Buyer visit First meeting	Coordinate due diligence
⇓	⇓	⇓	⇓
Data gathering Owner interview	One page business summary presentation	Tour business	Loan request package
⇓	⇓	⇓	⇓
Recast financial statements	Screen responses (financial quality of buyer)	Probe buyer interest	Lender introductions
⇓	⇓	⇓	⇓
Prepare valuations report	Determine buyers interest	Motivate buyer to act **Offer to purchase**	Assist in resolving all issues
⇓	⇓	⇓	⇓
Obtain listing agreement	Obtain CA Non Disclosure Agreement	Facilitate negotiations	Definitive purchase agreement
⇓	⇓	⇓	⇓
Prepare CBR Data package	Prepare CBR Data package	Agreement in principle (LOI or offer to purchase)	Review final documents
⇒	⇒	⇒	⇓
			Close !

Which are the most common reasons for business sale failure?

Knowing in advance what difficulties to expect is important, so they can be avoided or overcome. The following diagram shows the key factor and they can carry different weight, depending on the nature of the business, framework, scale, location and momentum.

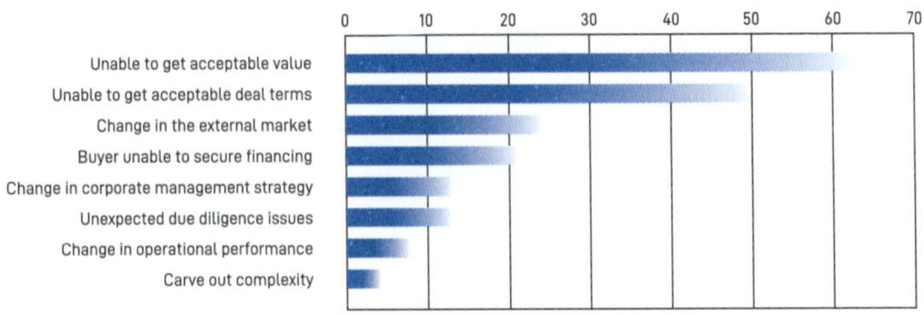

Source: Deloitte Divestiture Survey Report (2013) Reasons for not completing divestitures.

KEY IDEAS AND REFERENCES FOR MORE INFORMATION

- Selling or buying a business is complex and always requires rigorous evaluation
- Business evaluation is complex and with many influencing factors that require expert advice
- Evaluation is strongly influenced by tangible and intangible assets
- Knowledge about reasons for selling a business might be a relevant advantage in the negotiation process
- The business selling or buying follows a client-based logic and appropriate communication and information flow is critical

[1] Trugman, G. (2011) Understanding Business Valuation: A Practical Guide to Valuing Small to Medium Sized Businesses by the American Institute of Certified Public Accountants, Inc.

[2] Steingold, F.S. (0000) The complete Guide to Selling a Business. Nolo

[3] Poland, S. (0000) Founder's Pocket Guide: Startup Valuation, 1x1 Media.

[4] Chartered Business Valuation Institute, https://cbvinstitute.com

[5] Proffer, K. (2016) The Revised Art of War: Sun Tzu's Art of War revised for the 21st Century, Keiran Proffer.

[6] Lev, B. and Gu, F. (2016) The End of Accounting and the Path Forward for Investors and Managers, Wiley.

[7] Burlingham, B. (2013) Finish Big: How Great Entrepreneurs Exit Their Companies on Top, Portfolio.

[8] Haskel, J. and Westlake, S. (2017) Capitalism without Capital: The Rise of the Intangible Economy Hardcover, Princeton University Press.

21

Concluding remarks and key ideas

The Business Case Roadmap development is a never-ending process. The capacity to adapt to the ever-changing business environment is the main global factor for survival. It is of great importance to understand the process of evolving from the business idea to the business case (The BCR, Vol. 1); how to improve, test, validate and present the business case, and how to implement it (The BCR, Vol.2); how to master the multiple requirements and challenges during execution, and how to grow (The BCR, Vol. 3). Finally, it is also important to understand how to overcome the barriers for growth and how to navigate the financing process. Furthermore, it is fundamental to know how to avoid and/or manage mistakes and errors. Some key ideas from the BCR, Vol.3 can be described as follows:

- The business life cycle shows the past, the present and the future: growth is seen as a natural condition

- Growth strategies can be grouped into: organic growth (internal), with partnerships and with acquisitions
- Acquisitions can be of competitors, suppliers or related to strategies of differentiation
- Strategies may allow a shift from red ocean to blue ocean environments
- Investment is required for growth and might have many different forms depending on the context
- Investors, like any stakeholders, have "manageable profiles" that must be known
- Financing approaches may be grouped into grants and donations, a wide range of loans and different investment
- The investment arena is very complex and requires specific expertise and guidance
- Fast growth requires managing the comfort zone for all stakeholders
- Business longevity can be combined with growth and is part of the DNA and culture of organisations
- From gazelle and unicorn companies, we can learn about evolution patterns and trends, adaptable to any sector
- Hypergrowth requires bold leadership supported by skilled management
- Business failure can be avoided and managed when the related factors are known
- Business models are critical to avoid failure and develop added value business
- Sustainable growth requires going international and there are multiple options, starting with exports
- Value chain management is essential for international business

- Leadership, infrastructure development and communication are the main barriers to growth
- Continuous business evaluation and validation enables us to understand the strengths and weakness of businesses
- The business life cycle shows that a business should always be ready for sale
- Inspiring businesses that show sustainable growth teach us several things:
  1. They answer latent market needs
  2. They are internationally-minded right from the start
  3. They have knowledge as strong leverage
  4. They have managed to establish complete teams
  5. They were able to navigate the financial requirements

Luck is always an important factor in the success of business development, so...

More than good luck... we wish you

THE BEST POSSIBLE LUCK!